BIBLE MEDITATION

By the same author:
God Has Feelings Too

Bible Meditation

ALEX BUCHANAN

KINGSWAY PUBLICATIONS
EASTBOURNE

ISBN 0 86065 502 4

Unless otherwise indicated, biblical quotations are from the
New American Standard Bible © The Lockman Foundation
1960, 1962, 1963, 1968, 1971, 1972, 1973

NIV = New International Version, copyright © International
Bible Society 1973, 1978, 1984

Front cover photo: Photo Library International Ltd

Printed in Great Britain for
KINGSWAY PUBLICATIONS LTD
Lottbridge Drove, Eastbourne, E. Sussex BN23 6NT by
Richard Clay Ltd, Bungay, Suffolk.
Typeset by CST, Eastbourne, E. Sussex.

To
Ruth, Mark and Andrew:
my children
and
my friends.

Acknowledgements

In addition to those men and women mentioned in the preface, I would like to thank others who have helped, encouraged and suggested improvements for this book. These include Clive Calver, who first inveigled me into writing, and Richard and Shirley Harbour who, together with my wife, Peggy, and I, took on the Bible meditation course when Denis Clark 'changed his address'.

Contents

Preface

I would like to acknowledge the grace and patience of God towards me, and to pay tribute to several of those godly people who specially helped me to press on in my Christian life. Hence this brief testimony.

I grew up in a Christian home, and my mother taught me to read from the Bible when I was only three. My sister, Betty, and I went to Sunday school, and as a family we went to church wherever we lived. When I reached the age of thirteen I decided to leave religion to the women and children, and I went off with the lads. I got into trouble with the police and became a petty thief. I forgot all about God, but God did not forget me. A dear man, Leonard Tayler, had taken an interest in me earlier on. In fact, unknown to me at the time, he used to buy shoes for me because we were so poor, and later on he allowed me to clean his tandem for sixpence a week— a great privilege and an opportunity to indulge my lust for lollipops.

My first experience of conviction came when my sister and I spent our Sunday school offering on ice-cream. As we left the shop we saw Len coming along. The only thing to do was to stuff my cornet into my pocket, and, as he walked along with us, the fruit of my sin dripped steadily into my shoes together with my heart. This man pursued me, though I did not thank him at the time. God used him to make me think of spiritual matters again, but I still went my own way.

Then God allowed me to have an accident, the effects of which I still suffer today. It led to cerebral meningitis, a fractured skull, and radical mastoid. I became coma-tose. During a fleeting spell of consciousness I heard a doctor say to me, 'Son, we think you may have ten min-utes to live.' This frightened me to death, or rather to life, for it caused me to cry out to God for mercy, a cry which led eventually to my regeneration. I saw my first ever vision at this time. I saw two great gates which seemed to be made of solid light. They opened and I felt drawn between them. I saw something utterly indescrib-able, and I heard a voice saying very clearly, 'Not yet, my child, a little more rough tossing,' and then I felt myself drawn back from the gates. This experience raises two interesting points. First, at the time I was not God's child at all. How wonderfully he looks down the corri-dors of time and sees us in existence, long before we were ever born. Secondly, when I told my mother of this vision, she nearly passed out. 'Alex!' she exclaimed. 'I saw that same vision and heard those same words when I was dying from smallpox before you were born.' So, in God's mercy I was spared.

After the accident I went back to Glebe Hall in Ken-ton, a church which I had attended as a boy, where I heard the gospel again. One day, after I had been going for a few weeks, a man gave me a lift home. As I got out of his car he took my hand, shook it, and did not let go. 'Alex, are you a Christian?' he said. When I said no, he said, 'Remember that God's arms are wide open to you, why not run in?' So, quite simply, I did.

It was difficult to go on in my Christian walk at this time because I was quite sick, disfigured by paralysis, periodically stone-deaf, and blind for a short time. I staggered on from pillar to post, but in his love God enabled me to make some progress. It was at this time that I learned to meditate on the Lord. Quite frankly, I was such a wreck that very few wanted to build up a relationship with me. I could either have turned inwards and become bitter, or turned upwards and found God. In due course I recovered, and with the help of many people I grew as a Christian. Among these are Leonard Tayler, my father in God, Edwin Dawkins, an optician who opened my eyes to the need to study the word of God even more diligently, Alfred Dowton, who opened his home to me and made it a refuge, Alan Joyce who arranged for people to take notes of the messages when I was stone-deaf, and, of course, their wives who did not shrink from my deformed face, but loved and encouraged me.

I served the Lord in various places, and went to Matlock Bible College (now Moorlands), but I had a constant feeling that something vital was missing from my Christian life. Then I met my future wife, Peggy Sutherland, who was—and is—God's greatest gift to me, giving me comfort and confidence. However, she was also conscious of a deficiency in her spiritual life. God certainly used us, but when I looked at the New Testament Christians there was a great difference between their experience and mine. I did not see too many resurrections!

After years of secret heartache and desperate seeking, I met Denis Clark of Worthing, who became a great friend and colleague, teaching me much about intercession and Bible meditation. He came to the church in Matlock where I was an elder, and here I heard him speak about an experience of the Holy Spirit which I had always thought was of the devil. Denis brought great blessing to the town. One night in our house many people were prayed for and were transformed—but not me. I was furious with God, and cried out in utter frustration, 'Lord, this is just a load of rubbish!' God responded by graciously filling me with his Holy Spirit! I saw a vision of Jesus, tall and majestic, yet compassionate and near. I fell at his feet and fell gloriously in love with him—and have been ever since.

Following this experience came a time of deep depression, darkness and frustration. When you have tasted new wine everything else tastes like vinegar. My fellow elders did not understand my experience, putting it down to fanaticism. There was little, if any, understanding of the full work of the Spirit in their hearts. Doubt took hold of me and I languished. With hindsight I can now see that it is scriptural to be tested after a time of blessing, as Jesus was (Lk 4:1-14). Mercifully, God restored me and I regained the joy of that initial experience of the Holy Spirit's empowering and fullness.

My restoration gave me a great yearning to know the Lord more intimately, and therefore I ransacked the Bible to find those passages which to me, at any rate, spoke of him most clearly. I read them again and again, meditating on them closely, and as I did so I got to know him more deeply and love him more dearly.

It is the desire of my heart to help others find God and be used by him which has urged me to write this book. May it bless, challenge and inspire its readers as much as it has its author.

ALEX BUCHANAN
Chester 1987

Part 1

Bible Meditation

I

Not by Bread Alone

'Isn't meditation just an optional extra, a little frill to our prayer life?' some people may say. 'Do we really need to meditate?' We may as well ask if we need food, drink and fresh air. Try living without these and see! Spiritual life is at least as important as physical life, but it is not usually as well cared for. Food, drink and air will keep us physically alive for many years, but eternal, spiritual life has to be nourished from other sources, one of the prime ones being Bible meditation. Why don't we get our priorities right? So much time and trouble is taken over our temporal welfare, but not so much over the care of our eternal soul. Jesus said, 'Do not be anxious for your life, as to what you shall eat, or what you shall drink; nor for your body, as to what you shall put on. Is not life more than food, and the body than clothing? (Mt 6:25). Jesus was not unrealistic enough to suggest that we take no thought at all over our food and clothing, but he was saying that our priorities must be right.

Preoccupation with the affairs of this life is an enemy of Bible meditation, it leads to spiritual weakness and apathy. Anorexia Nervosa is a common ailment today, and there is a spiritual version of it from which many Christians suffer: a disinclination for and neglect of spiritual food, resulting in an emaciated spirit, a listlessness in activity, and a guilt complex due to the knowledge that deep down they should not and need not be as they are. Again, Jesus said, 'Man shall not live on bread alone, but on every word that proceeds out of the mouth of God' (Mt 4 :4). Living by the word means 'eating' it, or meditating deeply and repetitively on it. God says that we cannot live without having his words deep within our hearts, so it is vital that we eat and live, not just read and admire, his word.

My wife makes her own muesli, and apart from eating it she also uses it as an illustration when teaching about the faith. She says, 'I can tell you that there are lovely nuts in this muesli, as well as millet flakes, raisins, wheatgerm and oats. I can tell you that it will do you good: it will give you energy and maintain your health. But it will do you no good until you get a spoon and eat it!' Ezekiel would applaud her because he heard God say to him, 'Eat this scroll [God's word]' (Ezek 3:1), which he duly did, and was strengthened to speak out God's message to Israel. We may *exist* as Christians, but that is not what Jesus had in mind when he died for us. He said, 'I came that they might have *life*, and might have it *abundantly*' (Jn 10:10, my italics).

Ask yourself these questions: is Jesus an excitingly real person to me, as real as the one I love best on earth? Is the Bible a living, stimulating, enjoyable book to me? Am I living the joyful, abundant life which Jesus died to give me? Do I enjoy that spiritual energy which comes from devouring the Bible, making my Christianity vital and vigorous? If the answers to these questions are no, then you are in desperate need of the bread of God—you need to meditate on the word of God. You may need other things as well, for Bible meditation is not the only means of spiritual nourishment, but it is one of the most neglected.

Meditation is represented by various meanings in the original languages of Scripture. It means to consider or ponder (2 Tim 2:7); to eat or chew (Ezek 3:1); to observe or consider carefully and accurately (Mt 6:28; Heb 12:3); and to mutter (Josh 1:8).

Meditation is 'the art of being still before God, and allowing the Spirit to speak to us through the Scriptures, as we think over them slowly and carefully.' It involves 'chewing and digesting the Word until it gets from our head to our heart, thus affecting our will and conduct.' It has a clear purpose—it is what I call the 'thoughtful contemplation of God's Word in order to obey it.'

Other writers give the following definitions. Morton Kelsey writes: 'Meditation is the attempt to provide the soul with a proper environment in which to grow and become.'[1] Joseph Newton puts it this way: 'Every man has a train of thought on which he rides when he is alone. The dignity and nobility of his life, as well as his happiness, depend upon the direction in which that train is going, the baggage it carries, and the scenery through which it travels.'[2] William Ullerthorne observes: 'The acts of contemplation are four; to seek after God, to find Him, to feel His sacred touch in the soul, and to be united with Him and to enjoy Him.'[3]

There are many references in the Bible to the need of meditating on God's word, and the blessings of doing so. God warned Joshua that he would never be prosperous and successful unless he meditated day and night on the word of God (Josh 1:8). The Psalmist said that the person who meditates on the word is 'like a tree firmly planted by streams of water, which yields its fruit in its season. And its leaf does not wither. And in whatever he does, he prospers' (Ps 1:3). The patriarchs are said to have 'walked with God', including Enoch (Gen 5:22);

Noah (Gen 6:9); Abraham (Gen 17:1); Eleazar (Gen 24:40) and Isaac (Gen 48:15).

When it implies, in Genesis 17:1, that Abraham obeyed the command of God that he should walk before him, I wonder how he did this? I can't imagine that it simply means Abraham continued to live; I believe that he and God had a lot to share with each other. Abraham must have often meditated on God's word to him that he should possess the land and have a son in this old age, and also on the implications of substitution after Mount Moriah. Moses spent six weeks on Mount Sinai with God on at least one occasion. Was it spent only in continuous, uninterrupted prayer? I don't think so. I believe that he spent much of this time contemplating the glory of God and the beauty of his handiwork in creation. Indeed, it may well have been this experience which caused him to cry out to the Lord to show him his glory in greater reality. In our day, too, we can meditate on the Scriptures, as well as on creation. Whether Scripture was available to Moses before he wrote the Pentateuch, I do not know, but certainly creation was his inspiration.

Did God give Moses the ten commandments just once verbally, or did Moses need to meditate on them until he was word perfect, I wonder? It could well have been necessary for him to meditate long and often on the glory of God and his ways (Ps 103:7) as part of the preparation for writing the Pentateuch. God certainly inspired the word, but he used men to write it down, and those men needed to be made sensitive enough to understand exactly how God wanted it written.

David spent his boyhood as a shepherd out in the open, away from the distractions of the cities. He must have had plenty of time to meditate on creation and the one who made it. Perhaps it was during this time that he first realized that 'the heavens are telling of the glory of God; and their expanse is declaring the works of His hands' (Ps 19:1). Reading the Psalms gives a vivid impression of a man steeped in Bible meditation. Although David fell into sin with Bathsheba after seeing her from his roof-top, I believe that that roof-top was also the place where God communed with this 'man after His own heart' (1 Sam 13:14). God had much to share with him, and David gave God the chance to do it. The result is a compendium of instruction in righteousness, cameos of Christ, a history of Israel, splendid prophecies, comfort, rebuke, exhortation and a revelation of God's own heart. All this, because he knew how to meditate on the Lord.

I should imagine that when Ezekiel lay on one side for a long time as a demonstration on God's behalf to Israel, he spent much time meditating on the nature of the one who called him into the fellowship of his sufferings. Indeed, I would think that he needed to do so in order to keep his reason!

I wonder what Jonah was doing in the belly of the great fish? Jonah 2:7 says, 'While I was fainting away, I remembered the Lord; and my prayer came to Thee.' I believe that Jonah knew something about Bible meditation, and that he was earnestly contemplating his Lord at that time. Remember, he was a prophet and would have known the Scriptures extant at the time, so the great fish wasn't the only one with plenty to chew over!

Paul, in the desert for three years, must have gained much of his revelation through meditating on the scrolls which he must have taken with him to read. It may well have been during that time that he realized the true nature of the one whom he had formerly only known theoretically. Perhaps, too, his meditations put him in a right frame of mind to receive God's inspiration to write his epistles.

Chief of all these great people who were given to Bible meditation is our Lord Jesus—the one at whom the

Father looked and was so thrilled with what he saw that he decided to fill the earth with millions like him. We need to meditate upon him in a disciplined way if we are to be like him. God will not transform us without any effort on our part. If we really long to enjoy the full benefits of meditation, if we want to prosper in the things which do not fade away, then we must join the multitude of people in all ages who have obeyed Paul's exhortation to Timothy that he should pay close attention (meditate on) the truth he teaches (1 Tim 4:16).

Apart from those people mentioned in Scripture, many in more recent times have understood the importance of Bible meditation. I think of those such as Amy Carmichael, whose beautiful poetry, rising out of her meditations on the word, blesses so many of us today. Frances Havergal wrote her wonderful hymns after much time spent in the Scriptures. Saintly Robert Simpson said in his last week on earth that 'the Lord had been preaching to him better than a hundred sermons'. Brother Rieves asked him what it was. He said he had been meditating about the Israelites' servant in Exodus 21:5-6, who when given the chance to be free, refused that freedom because he so loved his master. 'Now,' said Bro. Simpson, 'I have served my Master so long, and I love my Master still; and if I were to live a hundred years more, I would not leave my Master, and upon the resolution the Lord came in upon my soul, and said I should be His servant forever.' George Mueller was another man much used of God who spent time in meditation.

The fruits of meditation are precious to God. The Psalmist says, 'Let the words of my mouth and the meditation of my heart, be acceptable in Thy sight, O Lord' (Ps 19:14). How marvellous that we can give the one who owns everything a present which he really enjoys—the fruit of our Bible meditations, and the kind of worship ensuing from this. However, we actually have to meditate before we can give him what he desires. How much do we really want to give God a present? Psalm 63:6 says, 'I meditate on Thee in the night watches.' Even when we are not sleeping well we can chew over the word of God and it will affect us.

Creation should be a stimulus to our spiritual life. Psalm 77:12 says, 'I will meditate on all Thy work.' Stars, flowers and mountains have all inspired worship as people have meditated on their beauty and perfection. However, meditation on the created universe should always be combined with meditation on the word of God in order to keep our hearts focused in the right direction. Psalm 119 reflects this.

Above all, meditation creates within us a deep yearning for God, a greater longing to know him, love him and find ourselves in him. David wrote: 'I meditate on all Thy doings; I muse on the work of Thy hands. I stretch out my hands to Thee; my soul longs for Thee, as a parched land' (Ps 143:5).

Meditating on the Scriptures is an ancient discipline, and one which God is re-emphasizing today. It has been much neglected by evangelicals, though not by Anglo-Catholics and some other Christian traditions. It is a wholesome and God-ordained way of bringing relaxation to the spirit, which in turn brings peace to the entire being.

Meditation is not a mystique, nor a quick way to instant holiness. It is not complicated, and it is not only for the spiritually advanced. It has to be exercised in a careful way, but it is one of the most beneficial of the spiritual exercises. It should be an integral part of our fellowship with God and thus of our prayer life, which will be greatly strengthened by it. It is one of the main ways in which God speaks to us, and is a means of training our inner ear to listen to him. Meditation helps us to really understand and be transformed by God's word, and to know God more deeply. It enables us to feed others with the truth too. It is also the best foundation for prophecy (discussed later in depth). Contemplating the word eases strain and stress, opening the way for the peace of God to enter our innermost heart. It is one of God's greatest ways of healing, calming and strengthening his people, and one of the greatest ways of maturing in our spiritual life and understanding. The art of meditation has been seriously neglected for far too long. It is now our responsibility to learn about it and reintroduce it to the whole of the church.

Pause and ponder

If Bible meditation is a way of working together with the Holy Spirit, surely I should be learning it.

2

The Discipline of Bible Meditation

Bible meditation is one of the most important ways to spiritual maturity, it is true. However, it is not a short-cut to holiness. Although it is a simple discipline, and even the weakest saint can learn it, it is not easy—nothing valuable ever is. Discipleship is impossible without sacrifice and discipline.

Time after time Jesus spelled out the cost of the cross to his followers. He called on them to deny themselves and to accept the rigours of prayer, constant instruction in the Scriptures, tiring preaching tours, separation from their families at times, and overcoming the flesh. Bible meditation, as part of our walk with the Lord, will be difficult at times; it will certainly be demanding. But what is the desire of our hearts? An easy life, or to know the living God? Those who truly love the Lord will have but one answer. Our feet should be on the rugged road which leads upwards. It is a mountain path, not an escalator. As an old hymn says: 'It was the path the Master trod, should not His servants tread it still?'

Some say that the Christian path is not a bed of roses. I both agree and disagree. In my earlier years, when I was ignorant of the dangers of the martial arts, I enrolled in a self-defence course. After I had qualified, I took on a man who was staying at a friend's house. I threw him twice quite easily; then it was his turn. My memories of the next few minutes are rather hazy, but I do remember landing in a bed of roses. Fragrant indeed were the petals, but the thorns had a very penetrating effect. How was I to know that he was a commando instructor? There is much in the Christian life which is fragrant and joyful, but there are also many painful lessons in store for those who would learn the key disciplines of the royal life to which God calls them—and he does not allow these disciplines to be easily learned.

Spiritual things are not cheap, they are much too valuable for that. Our access to them was accomplished for us by the costly sacrifice of Jesus at Calvary. In the light of that tremendous cost, how can God throw out gems of revelation cheaply, like spiritual smarties? If he did so, he would present to himself a bride who is a mere child, an army wrapped in cotton wool, a family of spoiled brats. Such a people would never impress the angels, and neither would they satisfy the God who is determined to have a people who 'attain to the unity of the faith, and of the knowledge of the Son of God, to a mature man, to the measure of the stature which belongs to the fulness of Christ' (Eph 4:13).

Such a glorious destiny demands that we devote our best energies to preparation for it, not the fag-end of our day or the remnants of our concentration. God is a very purposeful person. He is always doing something and going somewhere. His mind is teeming with great plans and intentions. There is nothing small about this God, how then could he be satisfied with small people in his kingdom? Weak we may be, but small we need not be. God promises us that 'he who began a good work in you will perfect it until the day of Christ Jesus' (Phil 1:6), for 'faithful is He who calls you, and He also will bring it to pass' (1 Thess 5:24). If we are willing to follow him, then he is willing to enable us to do so. If we will meditate on his word, then he will reveal himself to us in it. God is intent on his plan to transform us into a wonderful people, but because of his divine courtesy he waits for us to co-operate with him in its fulfilment. Bible meditation is one way in which we can lovingly do so. It is not an easy path, but it is a gloriously fruitful one.

Pause and ponder

If Jesus meditated on the word despite distractions, then I can learn to do likewise. All God looks for in me is willingness. I can start today, confident of promises that he will help me.

3

Perils along the Path

Before setting out on the discipline of Bible meditation, we should be aware of the possible dangers. By 'danger', I do not mean the terrible, mind-destroying danger of the meditation practised in some cults. The perils of Bible meditation lie in how we carry out the discipline, how we relate it to other aspects of our Christian life, and how we view it.

When pondering over one particular passage of scripture, it is easy to overemphasize one aspect of the truth at the expense of another, which may eventually lead to serious doctrinal error. For example, we can over-emphasize the grace and love of God at the expense of his holiness and anger, if we fail to meditate equally on both. John 14 does not say that Jesus was full of grace and love, but full of grace and truth—both must be kept in fine balance. A lovely illustration of these two aspects of his character is found in the story of the woman taken in adultery (Jn 8:3-11). Grace was seen in that he did not condemn her as the scribes did; truth was seen in that he sternly warned her to sin no more.

Taking Scripture out of context can be dangerous. A

friend of mine once took the passage in Numbers 13:17-24 and concluded from it that he should go southwards and that it should be at the time of grape harvest because the bunches of grapes mentioned in verse 23 meant that it was grape harvest time. On the basis of this, he went to a warm country when it was grape harvest there. He did not check this against other scriptures, nor with his leaders, nor did he pray about it. When he got to the warm country, some Christians took him around and announced him as a celebrity all over the land. Pride crept in, financial problems arose, and invitations ceased. He backslid and ended up out of the will of God.

For many people Revelation 3:20 is a favourite verse to meditate on, and some use it as a gospel text, but it is in fact a stern message to God's people. Undoubtedly some people have been saved through it, but the church is imperilled if she ignores the fact that God is waiting to enter her doors. We must not take Scripture out of context.

We cannot live on a diet of precious thoughts and spiritual titbits: another danger in Bible meditation. The Bible is a well-rounded book, and only those who devour it all can be well-rounded Christians. Many people use promise boxes, but I would advise their use solely to help memorize Scripture, and not as a sort of spiritual bran tub out of which we may magically find guidance.

We can tend to despise Bible study instead of realizing that it is an essential part of Bible meditation. Those who fall into this trap often overstress the need to 'rely on the Spirit', rather than to prepare careful notes.

Another danger is that of élitism, in which those who have learned something about Bible meditation adopt a superior attitude to those who have not. Such folks may hive off into a 'club' and become a pain in the pastor's neck. False piety can mar an otherwise good testimony and destroy genuine fellowship.

As we meditate in God's presence, we should always be aware of becoming overfamiliar with God by dwelling too much on his love and grace. Yes, *abba* does mean daddy, and the father heart of God is wonderfully tender, but God's tenderness is never at the expense of his holiness. The Psalmist poses an important question when he asks: 'Who may ascend into the hill [presence] of the Lord?' The answer is a salutary one: 'He who has clean hands and a pure heart' (Ps 24:3-4). Although we do not have to go through the awesome ritual demanded of the High Priest in Israel, before he went just once a year into the Holy of Holies, and although we are able to go boldly to the throne of grace, we cannot go lightly to that holy place.

If familiarity breeds contempt, then let us beware of familiarity. If Bible meditation becomes the all-absorbing thing in our lives, let us beware of imbalance. If pride has crept in, let us confess it. The Christian pathway contains many dangers, but through encountering and overcoming them we become mature (Heb 5:14).

Pause and ponder

Should I neglect Bible meditation because of its possible dangers? Or should I press on with it, trusting God to guard me as I do so?

4

A Warning Note

This book is not about meditation, but *Bible* meditation. This is a very necessary distinction because of the inrush into our country in recent years of Eastern religions and philosophies, many involving mystical meditation. Many sincere Christians are unwittingly dabbling in this by going to various exercise and relaxation classes, or learning certain types of martial arts—all of which are being rapidly absorbed into our culture and seem superficially harmless. Let's look at one or two of these and contrast their form of meditation with that revealed in the Bible.

Yoga

The physical exercises cannot be separated from the mental part; to be involved in either is participation in Hinduism. Mrs Mac Tompsett, an ex-yoga teacher known to me, has this to say:

> *Yoga* means 'to yoke', indicating a union of the individual soul to the universal soul (Brahma). Some people feel that the exercises are harmless, but for a Christian they are not.

Some are 'moving' mantras (prayers to deities), and others are designed to stimulate energy centres in the body to induce enlightenment. Yoga is progressive, affecting the way one thinks and feels. It teaches that there are many ways to God who dwells within everyone, and also teaches the doctrine of reincarnation.

Despite all this, yoga seemed just right for me: a non-competitive exercise programme with meditation and relaxation. As a mother with two exhausting children, I was desperately feeling the need of something for myself. One evening class a week seemed harmless. Our teacher occasionally gave us snippets of yogic philosophy which I dismissed when they conflicted with my Christian commitment. Later I attended a tutors' course and qualified with the All India Board and the Wheel of Yoga diplomas.

Slowly my ability and opportunity to witness for the Lord Jesus was lost. Time for Bible study and prayer was eroded as I became immersed in yoga and the needs of students. At further seminars we received teaching on philosophy and Buddhist meditation. One day the Holy Spirit asked me how Jesus would feel if he found me in this situation when he returned. From then on there was civil war in my mind. I tried to bargain with God, but I realized that I must surrender my will. Yoga teaches that sin is an illusion, ignorance or unreality which can be peeled away like an onion skin, but I knew that the Bible teaches that sin is real and that it must be confessed and can be forgiven. It took a vision of the Lord himself finally to convict me. I saw his face as he hung on the cross for me. His eyes showed no condemnation, just pure love and sorrow. I said yes to him, and was delivered. Subsequently, I saw several former students come to the Lord, praise his name.

T.M.

Transcendental Meditation may easily ensnare some Christians who are not well grounded in the faith. They say that they only attend classes to learn how to meditate, little realizing how adept the devil is at introducing

subtle error in the guise of apparent good. The meditation aspect of T.M. looks harmless, even good to them;
they reason that they can be strong against any 'harmful'
elements if they come across them. However, T.M. is a
religion; it is a modernized version of an ancient Vedic
aspect of Hinduism. Although described as a science by
its gurus, I believe that its real aim is to popularize the
Hindu scriptures. The fact that it is directed to Brahma,
the Hindu deity underlying all existence, together with
its belief in reincarnation, is proof that it is a religion.
The initiation ceremony is conducted by a priest, with
prayers and incense offered to gods, and in the Sanskrit
language so that few Westerners can follow it properly.

T.M. plainly contradicts God's law that we should
have no other gods beside him (Ex 20:3). Certainly, the
hold of T.M. is a stranglehold. Some who have been
ensnared by this cult say that it is an evil, brainwashing
thing, so strong that when they came out of it they
needed spiritual deliverance from the power of demons.
It has been reported that death threats were made
against some who left it; others were ensnared by the
occult aspect, only known when the 'higher levels' are
reached. Yet T.M., among other cults, is being offered
to our police force as a means of reducing strain, and
some are advocating that it should be offered on the
National Health Service. I believe this to be yet another
aspect of the devil's infiltration of Britain in order to
destroy it as a nation.

Such forms of meditation focus on self-discovery, self-
fulfilment, and, in some systems, the achievement of
nothingness, whereas God wants the focus to be on his
Son and our fulfilment of the glorious destiny which we
have in and with him. Satan counterfeits everything God
does, therefore it is not surprising that when he sees
some of God's people rediscovering the lost art of Bible
meditation, he uses Eastern cults and their gurus in

order to create confusion about the whole issue of meditation. Those who learn to meditate deeply in the Bible become more dangerous to the devil, therefore he will stop at nothing to side-track us from it. Bible meditation has nothing to do with mantras, centring down, postures or any of the trappings of what are basically evil cults. It has no gurus and only one focus—the Bible and its glorious author, the only true God.

Martial arts

There is reason to be suspicious of these arts because of the subtle religious connotations in many of them. Many Christians send their daughters to martial arts classes and the like in order to enable them to defend themselves against rapists. This is very understandable, but many instructors admit that a lone woman, even though she practises a martial art, is unlikely to overcome a determined attack from a strong man. She would need to spend many years practising to have any chance at all.

Another reason for being suspicious of these arts is the fact that most of them originated in an ancient religion.

I have culled some thoughts here from Mike Taylor's book *Martial Arts: Are They Harmless?* (Diasozo Trust).

The so-called 'masters' of these believe that there is a 'spiritual world' which can be tapped into and used by performing the activities relevant to the arts. This is true of all those connected with yoga, Zen and Tao, on which all the martial arts are based. Tapping this supposed 'spirit world' requires a form of meditation intended to 'still the thought processes, in order to experience altered stages of consciousness, leading to spirit mediumship'. The masters insist on implicit obedience, suspension of all other judgement, and practice of what they specify. They gradually take the students on to

31

'higher levels' as they obey. Those following such instructions begin to feel that they are in command of special powers (sometimes called the power of *ki*), but this is the deceptive part of the whole thing—they are actually in the power of the demons behind these systems. These demons do indeed give power of a sort to enable men to accomplish things beyond the normal, but the devotee surrenders his soul in exchange. Not all feats by karate practitioners come into this category, for some are done by heightened agility and strength brought about by sheer practice, but many feats go well beyond that, and it is to these that I allude. One 'wing chun' practitioner 'punched' a man from nine feet away, severely hurting him. Was that normal? The fact that martial arts seem to work beneficially for some is a delusion. They *seem* to work, because demons have deluded practitioners into believing that they are greater than before. Where systems have roots in the occult, the people of God cannot have anything to do with them if their spiritual lives are to be kept intact. I have counselled many Christians in deep despair, and many of them were only delivered when they confessed and renounced their involvement in these 'arts'.

All the above mentioned forms of meditation are dangerous and should be avoided. No Christian should have anything to do with systems which are in any way connected with false religions.

5

Meditation in the Modern Age

Is Bible meditation really possible, or even practical, in this modern age? Does it really have an important place and valuable contribution in this frenetic, high-speed, deadline-dominated era in which we live? My answer is yes, if we really want to know God better than we do. In fact, Bible meditation is vital, simply *because* of our frantic times. I believe that it is utterly realistic to meditate on the word. If we want the same divine economy seen in the life of Jesus who said, 'Whatever the Father does, these things the Son also does,' and again, 'As I hear, I judge' (Jn 5:19, 30), then we must meditate as he did. Although Jesus was the Son of God, he still needed to meditate day and night on the Scriptures. He would have been familiar with Joshua 1:8: 'This book of the law shall not depart from your mouth, but you shall meditate on it day and night.' If that was true of him, then it is certainly true of us.

Jesus not only read this command of his Father, he obeyed it. We have to ask ourselves the question, 'Do I *want* to learn to meditate, or do I merely *wish* I could?' Expert musicians and athletes did not attain their expertise by wishing they could become expert in their field, they got down to it because they really wanted to excel. Should the sons and daughters of God himself be less devoted to an exercise that has such eternal consequences? As Paul observed: 'Everyone who competes in the games exercises self-control in all things. They then do it to receive a perishable wreath, but we an imperishable' (1 Cor 9:25).

Many different people can testify to the fact that it is possible to meditate on the word today, even in a very busy life. I know one lady who is a housewife with five demanding children, a husband with a taxing job, and pets galore. She also runs a wives' group. She gets the children to memorize Scripture with her, thus helping it to sink into her own mind. She then ponders it during the vacuuming of the carpets, noting her findings on one or other of the numerous note-pads about the place (with pen firmly tied to it!). During coffee break she meditates further and makes more jottings, and while peeling the potatoes she prays on the basis of her findings.

A businessman props a card with a verse on it against his shaving mirror and memorizes it while denuding his chin. On the drive to work he ponders it in-between traffic situations. He often scraps lunch and walks in a nearby park, meditating further and praying on the basis of this.

A factory worker walks to work and meditates while doing so. On his production line he has short periods of time during which he takes out a small card with a verse on it and begins to learn it. He reckons to a word of this for every car wheel he fits. Every other day he refuses to watch the TV news when he comes home, and instead spends extra time in the bath meditating and praying. I could mention many more, but let me just pick out some common factors from the above. All these people memorize the word; they all find some time, even if it is only a few minutes; they all use it; and they all mean business.

It is possible, then, to meditate today, but only by keeping two things in mind. One is our need of discipline and desire, the other is the help of the Holy Spirit. We do not have to be spiritual giants in order to meditate; in fact the more childlike we are, the easier it is for the Spirit to lead us into the riches of Scripture. He is abundantly able to do so, and he positively yearns to help us while we are still in the realm of time. He inspired men to write the Bible (2 Pet 1:21), so he is the expert we need. However, we are the only ones who can exercise our will. God could force us, because he can do all things, but he has decided never to override the human personality. Again, we must assess the strength of our desire; if it is strong enough we can do anything. If we really desire to be a pianist, scientist or lawyer, then we will give ourselves to the essential studies and practice which will enable us to achieve our objectives. Surely our desire to accomplish spiritual things should be at least as strong as that for earthly, fleeting pursuits.

While we are in the realm of time we can use time; in eternity we will not have the same kind of opportunity. It will be wonderful in heaven, but we will not be able to recall time and invest it again. If we say that we are too busy now to meditate on the Bible, it will not prevent us from getting to glory, but our rewards will be diminished. It is far better to make time and invest it in the word while we are alive. Perhaps heaven has never been real enough to us for the judgement seat of Christ to be an incentive to greater diligence in preparing for the exams which take place there. God desires the response of loving diligence and the joy of our co-operation. Let's respond by starting now!

Pause and ponder

I only have one life, but it is full of wonderful possibilities. If I am willing, God can save me from wasting it.

6

The Blessings of Bible Meditation

In this chapter I want to enlarge on the benefits and blessings of Bible meditation which are many and varied.

It helps us to see God

Bible meditation helps us see God as a real person. When I was first born again I had no great sense of God's nearness. I believed in him by faith, and in one sense he was real to me because I believed he is the eternal one, but he was a great Spirit rather than a vibrant person close by my side. In our relationship with God we should not depend on feelings, but neither should we be afraid of them. Christianity is, after all, a love affair, and God is not afraid to make his feelings known to us. Why shouldn't we desire to feel him close, and see his beauty and splendour?

When I speak of 'seeing' God I am not only thinking of visions, but seeing with the aid of Scripture. We will never see the complete glory of the Lord till we get to heaven. Our clearest visions will only be of his likeness, but that likeness is so glorious that it can leave one overwhelmed. Scripture records some of these instances, and we can see God more clearly by meditating on them. Isaiah saw the Lord and was overwhelmed (Is 6). Ezekiel wrote: 'Such was the appearance of the likeness of the glory of the Lord. And when I saw it I fell on my face' (Ezek 1:28). The Lord appeared to John on Patmos and he 'fell at His feet as a dead man (Rev 1:17). King David said in Psalm 16:8, 'I have set the Lord continually before me.' How did he do this? He was constantly meditating on the word, therefore he constantly 'saw' the Lord in it. David 'set' the Lord before him. 'Set' is a doing word, it speaks of determination and exercising the will. How can we see if we do not look? And how will we look unless we are determined to look?

These men wrote scripture under the guidance of the Spirit, but they must also have absorbed every bit of Scripture already extant in their times. Although it does not clearly state that these men were meditating at the time God revealed himself to them, I would strongly suggest that they were, and that if we do the same, we are at least likely to see something of God too.

It helps us to fall in love with God

Some might shy away from such language, saying that it is somewhat irreverent. But what is irreverent about love? A Christian who is deeply in love with God is not an idle dreamer, lolling about doing nothing, but one who is spiritually on fire and quickly obedient to every word he hears from the lips of his beloved Father. Bible meditation enables him to see the sheer beauty of God's holiness, the splendour of his grace, the generosity of his forgiveness, and the tender compassion in his heart. Understanding these things more and more as he meditates on such a God, he is bound to go around with a light in his eyes and a spring in his step, showing the world that he is a man in love. Others will ask him what is so special about his God, and he will gladly tell them.

It helps to make us like God

I wonder if you share the greatest passion of my own life, which is to be more like the Son of God? This is not an unreal objective, nor is it merely pious. We are only truly satisfied when we are like him; it was for this that we were born. This world will only change when God is seen in it, and I want to change it by showing him in and through my life to those around me. I may not do it very well, but I can at least try. I do not have much sympathy with those who are always beating their breasts and saying, 'Woe is me for I am a failure, God cannot use me.' God is far more bold than we think! He knew that we were weak and failing when he saved us, but he had plans and power, and he decided to use us and empower us to fulfil what he had in mind. We need all the help we can get, but we can get all the help we need—from God. However, we must do our part, for God will not do it all. Meditation is one way in which we should co-operate with him, and it will help us greatly in the glorious work of showing God to the world.

2 Corinthians 3:18 says: 'But we . . . beholding as in a mirror the glory of the Lord, are being transformed into the same image from glory to glory, just as from the Lord, the Spirit.' As Christians we are all Christlike to some degree, but we all have a long way to go. We want to be more like Jesus, but let us not forget to give God the credit and glory for what he has done in us already. We are too afraid of saying that we are like the Son of God; fear of pride looms large, and these fears rob us of legitimate joy. Satan has succeeded in creating within the church a false modesty, an embarrassment concern- ing these things, which causes us to speak of more

'down-to-earth' issues. It is possible to be expert in Bible exegesis but not necessarily have that deep and intimate knowledge of the one whom we serve. The Bible is not only a book, but a portrait of a real person whom we are intended to be like. Jesus said in his great prayer: 'The glory which Thou hast given Me I have given to them [us]' (Jn 17:22). Part of that glory is to be like him. To enable us to attain to this, God gave us his own life. Scripture talks of us becoming 'partakers of the divine nature' (2 Pet 1:4). Those who possess that life manifest their Father: like Father, like child. This surely means that we look like him, or at least, that we can and should do if we keep 'looking' at him by Bible meditation.

It deepens our fellowship with God

There are many aspects to fellowship with God, including prayer and evangelism. But Bible meditation is probably the most neglected area of our communion with God. Jesus' prayer 'that they may be one, just as We are one' (Jn 17:22) is often cited to underline the importance of church unity. But on what grounds is unity possible? Agreement on doctrine and practice alone will not bring it about, even if such agreement was possible across our denominations. I believe that the unity Jesus had in mind is that which comes about when Christians are so intent on their personal fellowship with God that nothing is allowed to stand in its way. If all the children of God are clustered around him, absorbed with his beauty and glory, and if they give themselves over to the Scriptures which describe his character, and if their great passion is to know him better, then there is true unity. For genuine, loving fellowship to exist, we must each have a close relationship with God in which we know him as a real, vital person. This can only happen if we constantly seek him and nurture our relationship with him. This will greatly help to make us one, as the God-head is one.

It helps us to endure

It is written of Moses that 'he endured, as seeing Him who is unseen' (Heb 11:27). But, you may ask, how does one see the invisible?

Moses spent many years in Egypt, learning its skills, enjoying its pleasures, and heading for high office. However, God had other ideas for him, so he transferred him to another class in Divine School—'40 D', or forty years in the desert. Here he had time to meditate on God, learn the value of remaining close to him, and prepare for leadership. His experience of the burning bush suggests that he had a lot to learn about God. He was afraid to lift his head when God spoke, he did not believe that he and God were a match for Pharaoh, and he almost laughed at the idea that Israel would listen to him. Even after God's wonderful promise and reassurances that he would be with him, Moses still did not believe that God's word could really be fulfilled. God, in his patience, gave him sign after sign of his power, yet he still argued with God and resisted his commands, pleading that he was not eloquent enough to convince Pharaoh or Israel. Eventually, when Moses said, 'Please send someone else,' God grew angry and gave him Aaron to go with him. Little did Moses know how great a hindrance his brother would be later on. If we think we are slow to learn in knowing God, even after our meditations, we should take courage from Moses who, although slow, yet spoke to God face to face (Ex 33:11).

Later on, Moses was to be the leader of about two million awkward, grumbling, treacherous people on a journey which beggars description. His own brother and sister, Aaron and Miriam, turned against him: Aaron turned the people to idolatry, and Miriam led a campaign against his leadership. He had to feed millions, find them water, offer the proper sacrifices for them without fail, maintain his prayer life, find revelation for every step of the way, and maintain his own family life—all this in the midst of dust, heat, noise, the bleating of thousands of sheep, and the rigorous physical demands made on him. His 'quiet times' must have been interesting! But they were surely times when he 'saw' the invisible God by meditating upon him. The cry of Moses' heart, 'I pray Thee, show me Thy glory' (Ex 33:18), indicates his hunger to know and see the Lord, and the statement in Exodus 33:11 that 'the Lord used to speak to Moses face to face, just as a man speaks to his friend' shows how God responds to a heart like that of Moses. It indicates that Moses saw the Lord not only (perhaps) in visions, but also as he thought over all that God must have said to him.

A man in Moses' position could only have endured all the events described in Exodus by constantly contemplating the Lord. None of our trials come anywhere near those of this man who was 'very humble, more than any man who was on the face of the earth' (Num 12:3), but it is still true that we will not endure unless we adopt the same habit of life seen in Moses.

I would like to enlarge on this matter of endurance, or perseverance, both in meditation and in prayer, because it is so important. I often wonder if the eleventh commandment could be, 'Thou shalt bash on'! Time after time, God exhorts us to press on. Paul urges, 'Pray at all times' (Eph 6:18), not sometimes. Again, in Luke 18:1, Jesus said, 'At all times they [men and women] ought to pray and not to lose heart.' Prayer is not an optional extra. I like the marginal reading of Luke 18:5 in the NASB: 'Yet because this widow bothers me, I will do her justice, lest by continually coming she hit me under the eye.' Delightful! And it was Jesus who told this story. He admires anyone who will press on and not be deterred. Luke 11:5-10 contains a similar story to encourage perseverance in prayer. The marginal reading of verse 8 in the NASB is as follows: 'And I tell you . . . because of his shamelessness, he will get up and give him as much as he needs.' Again, unashamed perseverance pleases God.

If we have failed in prayer or Bible meditation, let us heed the injunction in Hebrews 12:12 to 'strengthen the hands that are weak and the knees that are feeble'. Stop limping along the path to the celestial city. Get into some holy exercise again, toughen up and get moving! When God sees you doing this he will come right in with the help you need. Although I will be writing about prayer later in this book, the following extract on persevering in prayer is relevant to the discipline of meditation too.

> We are not only to pray without ceasing, but also without fainting (Lk 18:1). The first lesson is a warning against fitfulness in prayer, the second against lack of perseverance in it, both these failings ensnare many. No temptation in prayer life is more common. We begin to pray for a certain thing for a day, week, month; but receiving no answer, we faint and cease praying for it. This is a deadly fault. It is simply the snare of many beginnings with no completions and therefore ruinous. The man who forms the habit of starting without finishing has simply formed the habit of failure in prayer. To faint is to fail. Then defeat begets disheartenment and lack of faith in the reality of prayer, which is fatal to success. It is better to put up fewer prayers and get more answers than to have on hand a host of unfinished petitions with all the spiritual demoralisation that flows therefrom.[4]

It maintains purity

Satan has marred and despoiled the beautiful world

which God made for his, and our, enjoyment. Not only did he contribute to God's cursing its vegetation and making nature 'red in tooth and claw', but he has also brought about a change in the heart of man so that out of it come 'evil thoughts, murders, adulteries, fornications, thefts, false witness, slanders' (Mt 15:19). It was not so originally. Adam and Eve spent much time communing with God, looking at him, talking to him, responding to him, enjoying him. This kept them pure and whole until they took their eyes off the Lord and onto things.

Today we live in a broken, shabby world. It is hard to buy a newspaper without being faced with pornographic magazines. Many TV programmes are sadly spoiled by the intrusion of blasphemy and filth. Violence, hatred, injustice, acquisitiveness and envy are all evidence of the basic uncleanness pervading our world. But we live in this world. How, then, can we ever keep ourselves clean as we serve the Lord? Apart from obvious steps, such as switching off unhelpful programmes, we should follow the advice given in Psalm 119:9-11—'How can a young man keep his way pure? By keeping it according to Thy word. With all my heart I have sought Thee . . . Thy word I have treasured in my heart, that I may not sin against Thee.' One evidence that we treasure the word in our hearts is that we spend plenty of time meditating on it. If we are contemplating Jesus—his way of life, his thoughts, his attitude, the things he would look at, the things he would touch—our hearts will be filled with his purity. We watch him through our Bible meditations. I have already said that this is not easy, but it is worth the cost because it enables us to be like Jesus in a world which desperately needs to see him.

It feeds our spirit

No food, no life. What a gem of pure logic! But what is

true in the natural is also true in the spiritual. We were born again as spiritual babies, but we are not expected to remain as babies. Our spirit needs as much food as our body if we are to mature.

When Jesus taught us to pray, 'Give us this day our daily bread,' he implied spiritual bread as well as actual bread. But where is this bread to be found? In John 6:35 Jesus declares, 'I am the bread of life; he who comes to Me shall not hunger,' and in verse 56 he continues, 'He who eats My flesh and drinks My blood abides in Me, and I in him.' It is upon Jesus that we must feed if we would be spiritually alive and well. I believe that Jesus deliberately chose the imagery of eating and drinking here to emphasize how totally and completely we need to root ourselves in him to know spiritual maturity. We always need to be thinking of him, getting to know him, revelling in him, being heartened by who he is and what he has done, and taking advantage of it by receiving his forgiveness, grace, encouragement and love. As we meditate on Jesus in the pages of the Bible, we will know 'truth in the innermost being' (Ps 51:6).

It enables us to feed others

Old Mother Hubbard has her counterparts in some churches today. There's certainly a cupboard, with shelves and even a door, but no food for the family. The sermons are dry as dust, and the preachers are boring. Even if we as individual Christians manage to get food from the word, it is possible that we only get enough to keep ourselves alive, with none to spare for others. How utterly selfish! And what a shock when others come to us for help! Jesus told the story of the man taken by surprise when his friend called needing bread. In the East it was disgraceful to be unable to give hospitality. We in the West today could fall down here, too, in our inability to provide spiritual food for others.

Scripture is full of exhortations to help others, including feeding them. Isaiah 58:7 tells us to 'divide your bread with the hungry', and verse 10 continues: 'If you give yourself to the hungry, and satisfy the desire of the afflicted, then your light will rise in darkness.' James 2:15-16 exhorts us to feed, warm and clothe the needy ones among us, and not just talk about it. These exhortations can also be extended to spiritual food. If you have been meditating on the Lord in his word, you may be able to feed others with the fruit of this, strengthening them and lifting them up through words of Scripture, or through a prophecy. Get ready then! Respond to Jesus who said, 'Feed my lambs' (Jn 21:15, NIV).

It gives a basis for prophecy

There is much so-called prophecy about today, but a lot of it is trivial and tends to degrade the gift and put off those who are looking for the real thing. The best prophecy comes from those who have meditated long and often in the Scriptures. Their prophecies tend to ring true because they carry a certain authority with them, and do not contradict the word of God, but underline it beautifully. They may sometimes bring instruction about situations not mentioned in Scripture, but they will never go against the tenet of the Bible.

Pause and ponder

If Bible meditation brings so many vital benefits, how can we possibly neglect it?

7

The Brass Tacks of Bible Meditation

We've already looked at the difference between Bible meditation and that of some Eastern cults and considered some of the pitfalls as well as the benefits. But what is actually involved in the process of Bible meditation? Bible meditation is a discipline, and will therefore be easier for some than others because of our different temperaments. But we must learn the vital lessons involved if we are to succeed in meditation. If we are determined to learn, the Spirit is willing to help, so the word 'impossible' must be banished from our vocabulary.

Switching the mind

The mind is like a horse: it must be broken in, and then guided by reins into a certain direction dictated by the rider. Our minds are given to us by God and he will help us to use them well, but he will not force our minds into action—he leaves the direction to us. Lazy minds are easily taken over by the devil, disciplined minds are not. We have to learn not to be distracted by taking a firm

47

hold on the 'reins'. We will not be very successful in switching or controlling the mind unless we have something to switch it to, hence the importance of setting some aims at the start of the day. If we single out a verse or theme in the morning and memorize it, we will have something to turn our mind to when the need arises. If that focus is a verse which speaks of Jesus, and we switch our mind to it, then we will indeed 'turn our eyes upon Jesus'.

The next step is to combine switching the mind with learning to make full use of just a few minutes' time. Our dream of long hours of uninterrupted quietness in which to meditate will remain just a dream for most of us. But during the day everyone has a few moments in which we do something mechanically, such as peeling potatoes, washing the car, drinking coffee, or mowing the lawn. If, during these times, we can learn to switch our mind to the verses we focused on earlier and chew them over for a few minutes, then we will not only receive blessing from them, but we will be better able to use the hours, if and when we get them or can make them.

Reading

It may seem fairly obvious that Bible meditation demands Bible reading, but this is not always stressed in today's churches. Certainly, we must not fall into the trap of bibliolatry (virtual worship of the book itself), but neither should we try to live the Christian life with only a scant knowledge of Scripture. I have been deeply moved by hearing of the way in which God is bringing people to repentance in China and helping them to grow, even though many of them do not possess a Bible. However, that is a result of his sovereign grace in special circumstances. In the UK we have plenty of Bibles, and we are therefore responsible to God to read our Bible, know it, and obey it. One great sign that we appreciate our privilege of having the Bible is that we read it.

How wonderful it is that God wrote to mankind! He not only wrote the word straight from his heart through godly men, but he preserved it through the centuries, even though the devil stirred up one after the other to destroy it. It has been banned, burned, despised and rejected, but when a sovereign God decides to preserve it, no one on earth or in the kingdom of darkness can prevent him. It was a costly business for those whom he called to work with him in its translation, printing and distribution. Those such as Wycliffe, Tyndale, Coverdale and many others were imprisoned, maltreated, burned alive, banished or hanged for their faithful work. Spare a thought, then, for these heroes and heroines who laid down their lives so that we could read, learn and inwardly digest the word of the living God. If they considered the sacrifice worth while in order to bring it to us, then we should at least consider it worth while to read it.

Many Christians, when questioned, would say that of course they read the Bible. In reality, however, they have only read parts of it. If you have not read it right through, watch out because when you get to heaven it could be very embarrassing when a man comes running up to you saying, 'Did you enjoy my book? My name is Nahum.' If God went to such lengths to write the Bible for us, it is an insult to him if we do not bother to read it. It is a love letter from him, not just a history lesson.

Years ago when my wife and I were courting, she was at a camp in Wales and I was at a camp in Devon. I missed her, but consoled myself by refereeing a football match in my inimitable style, which no one else would dream of copying. During the match someone brought me a letter and I recognized Peggy's handwriting on it. I did not put it into my pocket for future reference, but blew the whistle, cancelled the match, rushed off under the nearest tree, and sat down to devour the letter from my beloved. Again and again I read it, full stops included, because she wrote it.

We should have a similar attitude to reading the Bible, which comes from 'the Son of God, who loved me and gave himself for me' (Gal 2:20, NIV). He constantly exhorts us to read it. Isaiah 34:16 carries the exhortation to 'seek from the book of the Lord, and read'. Writing to Timothy, Paul says, 'Give attention to the public reading of Scripture' (1 Tim 4:13). In the opening words of Revelation, John says, 'Blessed is he who reads and those who . . . heed the things which are written in it.' The Psalms are shot through with exhortations to read, study, meditate on and obey the word of God. Jesus said, 'Man shall not live on bread alone [feeding his mortal body], but on every word that proceeds out of the mouth of God [feeding his immortal spirit]' (Mt 4:4). Jesus read the word day and night because he loved its author and because he was under no illusions as to the power of his adversary, the devil. Jesus overcame the evil one when he was tempted in the wilderness by using the word of God. We, too, can overcome Satan if we immerse ourselves in Scripture, so wonderfully described as the 'sword of the Spirit . . . the word of God' (Eph 6:17), for no evil power is a match for those so armed.

Let's stop making feeble excuses and buckle down to reading the whole word of God, any time, all the time. Strap it to the vacuum cleaner if necessary; read it to each other after meals if you are married; if you are single, read it to yourself, and remember that angels are listening, to say nothing of the Lord. Do absolutely anything that will help you keep up with this precious, sin-destroying word of the living God.

Have you ever thought of reading the Bible onto cassette? Do it as a family in turn, or as a church in turn, or with your best friend. Help those who are dyslexic or blind by reading it to them or recording it for them.

People often ask me which is the best version of the Bible to use. I advise them to try them all and see which is the most helpful, and I also warn them not to use a paraphrase for a working Bible. The Good News Bible, Living Bible, and perhaps J. B. Phillips are good for quick and easy reading. The New International Version is very popular and readable. But whatever version we use, it is wise to look at the credentials of the translators and find out if they are liberal in their theology, i.e. they do not believe in miracles, or question the virgin birth, or suggest that the Bible contains myths. The Amplified Bible is good for understanding the wide scope in the meanings of the Hebrew, Greek and Aramaic languages. Chain reference Bibles are good as long as they do not become a lazy person's Bible. The Authorized Version is beautifully melodious, and for older people it has a comforting familiarity, but it is rather archaic in language. The New King James Version seems to be an improvement on the old edition, and many of those who insist that the 'Received Text' is the only true version are very keen on it. The New American Standard Bible is a very good, possibly the best, working Bible. Despite the varying values of the different versions, it is very much a personal choice as to which you use.

If, after all your reading, you feel that very little sticks, don't worry. More sticks in your mind than you think; just bash on. If you get stuck in Leviticus, and start wondering just how much more fat and entrails are involved before chapter 27, try to remember that Jesus often quoted from it, and that there are as many pictures of him in it as there are in any other book of the Bible. For that reason alone, it is worth persevering with it.

Chapter and verse divisions were not in the original

texts, and were not inspired by God. They certainly help in finding our place and in memorizing verses, but they are not always in the right position, so don't be afraid to ignore them. 1 Corinthians 9:24-10:13, for example, is one complete section, but the chapter division interrupts it. The same is true of Colossians 3:18-4:1, and Hebrews 3:12-4:13, and 4:14-5:10. In Ephesians 1 it makes better sense to read the end of verse 4 as part of verse 5: 'In love He predestined us. . . .' Similarly, Titus 2:15 is really the start of chapter 3. And so we could go on.

Studying

We should not make too strong a distinction between Bible study and Bible meditation; they are different, but they overlap. Study tends to inform the mind about the truth of the word; meditation tends to get it down into the heart so that it becomes operative in the life.

God plainly commands us to study the Scriptures: 'Be diligent to present yourself approved to God as a workman who does not need to be ashamed, handling accurately the word of truth' (2 Tim 2:15). If God can find diligent workers skilled in the truth, he will entrust important work to them. The Bible can never be properly understood by reading alone: there is far too much in it for that. We must study it too. Jesus would have learned to read the Scripture at his father's knee, for this was required of all Jewish boys (Deut 6:7), but he surely studied it too. When he was questioning the teachers in the Temple when he stayed behind in Jerusalem, they were astonished at his knowledge of the Scriptures (Lk 2:47). A further proof that he studied diligently was his authority in teaching (Mt 7:29), his wisdom (Mt 13:54), and his ability to confound the very teachers themselves (Mt 22:34). Satan himself could not overcome Jesus, for he was too skilled in the Scriptures.

See how he used them in his defence by saying every time the enemy attacked, 'It is written' (Mt 4:4-11).

Why not follow Jesus' example, and study the Scriptures as diligently as he did. Then you will have a similar effect on the people around you, and will experience victory over the enemy too. Start by reading Mark, the simplest gospel, then go on to study it. Keep a note-book so that you do not lose any 'crumbs'. Share your gleanings with your leaders or mature Christian friends, and ask them to correct any mistakes. Keep going and you will eventually find that when you read a phrase it will remind you of other scriptures which you have read elsewhere in the Bible. You may have to start again in Genesis to find them, or use the marginal references, and it may take time, but what an investment!

A concordance is a very useful tool in Bible study and meditation. Strong's is the most complete, Cruden's is briefer, while Young's is helpful in that it divides each entry into sections which reflect the original Hebrew and Greek words. (Pray before you see the prices, but recall how much you pay for shoes.) A Bible dictionary is helpful too. The Bible is an Eastern book and a dictionary can explain Eastern customs and shed light on tricky passages such as Isaiah 9:6—'The government will rest on His shoulders.' This refers to an Eastern wedding. The bride comes, veiled, with her father holding a drawn sword over her head as a symbol of his rule and protection over her. During the ceremony, the groom takes her veil and puts it on his shoulder, signifying that the protection of and authority over the woman has now passed from the father to him, and the bride's father lowers his sword in assent. This is a lovely picture of our relationship with Jesus.

Lexicons can be useful if we need to know the tense in the original language, or the meaning of obscure words. Commentaries can be helpful too. One of the simplest commentaries is *What the Bible Is All About* by H. Mears (Ventura, CA, Regal Books, 1983). But don't run to them first—they are, after all, other men's thoughts. Of course, we need men of greater scholarship than our own to help us find our way through the more difficult passages in the Bible, but my plea is that we should not start with them, but get experience ourselves first. In this fast-food age, it is all too easy to try making a quick and easy meal of the word. We reason that although it is food for our soul, we can probably bolt it down and still benefit from it. Take time pondering over the word yourself first, asking God to illuminate it for you.

Memorizing

Today in the UK Bibles are available at any time. But what if they are taken from us? It has happened elsewhere, such as China, Nepal and Uganda. Why should Britain be immune? God is increasingly judging Britain because of her persistent sin, and the Bible makes it quite clear that 'God is not one to show partiality' (Acts 10:34). If our Bibles were confiscated or destroyed, how much of them would we remember? The answer is, no more than we had memorized beforehand. It is time to be realistic and to step up our memorizing of the word of God. Then, if we are imprisoned, we can feed on it, defend ourselves from the devil with it, minister comfort to others from it, and even preach it to our jailers as Paul did. If this seems alarmist, just consider history carefully and be prepared.

We may suffer from a poor memory, but that is no excuse for not trying to memorize the Bible. Any memory can be improved by practice, and the Spirit of God takes tremendous pleasure in helping God's children to memorize the word of their loving Father. After all, he gave us a memory in the first place! Give him a chance and see. We may not remember everything which we vaguely wish we could remember, but we can remember most of what we determinedly want to remember. Proverbs 7:3 says, 'Write them [the Scriptures] on the tablet of your heart,' i.e., engrave it, cut it deep into your heart, take time and trouble over it. Be encouraged by yet another one of God's promises: 'I will put My Law within them, and on their heart I will write it' (Jer 31:33). We engrave it and he engraves it. As in everything, there is God's part and ours; co-operation all the way.

A busy mother in my congregation once said to me, 'It's all right for you; you have plenty of time to meditate and study the Bible, and you have no distractions.' At the time I was a pastor and a city missionary, with a sick wife, three children, and the 'suicide' phone line permanently in our home, which did not leave too much spare time! However, I asked her to get me a postcard, which I cut into four pieces. I wrote the same verse on each part, and put one by the washing-up liquid, another by the well-used frying-pan, another by the clock, and the last by the phone. I then told her to use the few minutes while she washed up, or fried the burnt offerings, or even the seconds she spent looking at the clock to memorize the verse. We had the usual argument as to whether it is possible to learn anything in such fleeting moments, but she did read those little pieces of postcard, meditated on them, and got the truth into her heart. Today she is a different woman.

Memorizing Scripture does work. The great thing is to persevere. It took me three weeks to memorize 1 Corinthians 10:13 during the training sessions for the Billy Graham counsellors at Haringey, but I did it, despite suffering from amnesia for several months prior to this, and can quote it perfectly today. I confess that if Charlie

Riggs, who was in charge of counsellors' training, had said, 'Review it, review it,' just once more, I might have very graciously strangled him, but I thank God for his persistence now. We can memorize Scripture by muttering a verse under our breath at the bus-stop (which will alleviate the boredom of your fellow travellers). We can do it by singing the Scriptures set to music, or by asking the Holy Spirit to give us our own tune to Scripture. At all costs, let's get the Bible into our hearts. Only then will we know real change.

Perseverance

A Chinese proverb says, 'A journey of a thousand miles begins with one step.' New Christians reading this book may say, 'How can I cope with all these demanding disciplines?' The answer is, 'Start!' Much of the Christian life is lived in cold blood; God nowhere promises us an easy ride. We have to press on whether we like it or not. However, it is not all an uphill slog. God does say thrilling things to us; he does give transforming visions; he does give strength and joy as we press on. If we feel that too much is required of us, then let us read again in Philippians 4:13—'I can do all things through Him who strengthens me.'

Slacking off is one of the besetting sins of the church. Novelty seeking and quick attainment are what this modern age is all about. Perseverance is for the fanatic, and endurance is an outmoded concept. These attitudes have affected God's people, and it is time to call them back to noble objectives and to God-ordained disciplines.

Reading, studying, memorizing, listening and hearing, obeying and persevering are all equally important aspects of meditation, and we must maintain a balance between them. If we only study, we will only become students; if we only sit and think, we will only become thinkers; if we only memorize, we only become text machines. We must ask, and trust, the Holy Spirit to help us keep a balanced approach to meditation.

Pause and ponder

If earthly qualifications demand a lot of time and effort, why should we think that less is required in qualifying as ambassadors of God?

8

Where Do I Start?

New Christians faced with the challenge to know the
entire Bible might well feel the need of either miracles or
tranquillizers! There is, indeed, so much to learn in this
marvellous book. The Bible is simple enough for a semi-
literate tramp to find Christ through a partially understood fragment of it, and yet at the same time it is profound enough to fascinate professors and baffle translators. How, then, should ordinary mortals start meditating on the word of God?

A place apart

First, find a place where you know you can regularly
read and study the Bible. It is good to have a special
place if possible, but you shouldn't get too anxious about
it. If you are easily distracted, try to find the quietest
place possible, or as an extreme measure try earplugs—
after all, we have to be practical if we are going to learn
fundamental disciplines. I have known people who have
meditated in a chicken shed (empty!), an airing
cupboard, a loft, a tree house, a garden shed and a

boiler room.

Be a bit adventurous and hardy if necessary. If you only have a cold bedroom as an alternative to the lounge, wrap yourself in an eiderdown and tuck a hot-water bottle in with you. If you are a young person and your parents have the TV on all the time, then you will have to sacrifice comfort and try the attic. Why should we expect to be comfortable all the time when the Son of God himself had nowhere to lay his head, let alone the monopoly of a lounge. A lonely hilltop in the wilderness was frequently the only place where Jesus could find some peace and quiet, and the nights can be very cold out there. If he thought it important to meditate and pray, whatever the cost and wherever the place, then we must also follow his example, obeying the words of he who said, 'If any one wishes to come after Me, let him deny himself, and take up his cross, and follow Me' (Mt 16:24).

Read the word

Having decided on a place, establish when and roughly how long you will draw aside. Then start reading your Bible, either from the beginning to the end, or some of the Old Testament and some of the New in turn. If you do the latter, it is better to read a few chapters rather than a few verses. Read as fast as possible, you remember more that way. If you read too slowly, you can get discouraged by the time it takes you. As you keep reading, single out a book for study. I have already suggested the book of Mark because it is one of the simplest, but ask God to guide you as to the one best suited to you. I'm not convinced that he will choose Haggai for you straightaway! There are several good Bible reading schemes available, but avoid those which jump around the Scriptures too much, because this destroys the sense of continuity and can be very confusing.

George Mueller was thoroughly practical and orderly in his meditation on the Bible. He wrote:

My practice had been for at least ten years previously, as an habitual thing, to give myself to prayer after having dressed in the morning. Now, I saw the most important thing I had to do was to give myself to the reading of the Word of God, and to meditation on it, that my heart be comforted, encouraged, warned, reproved, instructed, and thus by means of the Word of God, whilst meditating on it, my heart might be brought into experiential communion with the Lord.

I began therefore to meditate on the New Testament from the beginning, early in the morning. The first thing I did, after having asked in a few words the Lord's blessing upon His Word, was to begin to meditate on the Word, searching as it were into every verse to get blessing out of it; not for the sake of the public ministry of the Word, not for the sake of preaching on what I had meditated on, but for the sake of obtaining food for my own soul.

The result I have found to be almost invariably this, that after a very few minutes my soul has been led to confession, or thanksgiving, or intercession, or supplication, so that though I did not, as it were, give myself to prayer, but to meditation, yet it turned almost immediately into prayer. When thus I have been for a while making confession, intercession or supplication, or having given thanks, I go on to the next words or verse, turning all as I go on, into prayer for myself or others, as the word may lead to it, but still continually keeping before me that food for my own soul is the object of my meditation. The result of this is that there is always a good deal of confession, intercession etc. mixed with my meditation, and that my inner man is invariably nourished and strengthened, and that by breakfast time, with rare exceptions, I am in a peaceful and happy state of heart.

Thus the Lord is pleased to communicate unto me that which, after, or at a later time, I found to become food for other believers, though it was not for the sake of the public ministry of the Word that I gave myself to meditation, but for the profit of my own inner man.[5]

As I have said before, a concordance is necessary for Bible meditation, so keep one handy so that you can trace other references to a particular word which interests you. Bible dictionaries are also helpful. Vine's *Expository Dictionary of New Testament Words* is a good one. Make sure you have your notebook at hand so that you can record what you find. Remember that when Jesus fed the crowd he did not waste the crumbs, so don't waste yours. Always ask the Holy Spirit to illumine the Scripture for you, for without his guidance you will glean nothing.

Start by reading and studying single words, including names of people, titles of God, and place names. Individual words yield a lot of fruit. Then go on to study phrases, verses and themes. Resource material to help you is given in Chapter 10.

Chew over the word

Once you have read the passage of Scripture, and maybe studied it, start chewing it over. If you gain only one tiny thought from your meditations, don't be discouraged— you won't master the Bible in one easy lesson! Those of us who are polite usually eat our meals one mouthful at a time; the size of the mouth does vary, but it is usually smaller than a dinner-plate! So, enjoy your spiritual mouthful and go back for more.

Don't be afraid to chew over the same thing for a week or so—it may take us a long time to understand and believe a certain scripture, but it is always worth persevering. It took me three weeks to believe the truth of Song of Solomon 4:9—'You have ravished my heart' (Revised Standard Version). Today many Christians are spiritual novelty seekers, for ever wanting something new. The average congregation looks to the leader for a new sermon every Sunday, but this doesn't mean that they remember what he said in the last one. It is said on good authority that one pastor preached the same sermon for a year, and when his deacons asked him when he was going to preach a different one, he said, 'When you have really grasped this one, then I will preach a new one.' Wise man! So, keep on chewing till you get the goodness to where it belongs—deep within your heart.

Apply the word

Bible meditation is not an end in itself; its purpose is to produce practical results in our lives. Therefore, as you progress, make sure that you really learn to apply what you have culled from the Bible. Consider how the truth touches on your day-to-day life. For example, if you have meditated on a verse which reflects the compassion of the Lord, ask him to show you how to be more compassionate to those close to you at home, and also to your colleagues at work, for they may never have experienced true compassion before. Perhaps you may meditate on the command: 'Do not lie to one another' (Col 3:9). Scrutinize your conversation—you might be in for a shock! When your friends ask you how you are, and you always respond, 'Fine, thanks,' it is possible that you are being less than truthful. After one of our Bible meditation courses some years ago, one of the students remarked, 'I know that I am different because I meditated on that verse and now I tell the truth.' As you press on, keep asking the question which my wife constantly asks in meditation seminars: 'How does this apply to me?' If it is a command that you are chewing over, ask yourself, 'Am I obeying this?' If you are not, then stop meditating, repent, and ask God to help you obey it. Then go back to meditating again. Bible meditation yields little to the rebellious!

Bible meditation not only produces practical results in our own lives, but also becomes a blessing to others as we learn to share the fruit of it. Don't bore people by constantly enthusing about your personal insights, but don't give way to fear of what others will think or the inverted pride of thinking that you will sound super-spiritual. Bible meditation is not a mystique. Learn how to introduce it to others in a sensitive way.

Pause and ponder

With so much ground to cover, and so much fruitfulness to be gained, shouldn't I be getting down to Bible meditation straightaway?

9

Help!

God never ignores a genuine cry for help. 'The eyes of the Lord are toward the righteous, and His ears are open to their cry' (Ps 34:15). He is a responsive God; a God with a heart, able and willing to enable us to live according to his plans for us. Whenever he commands us to do something, he enables us to obey. However, he does wait for us to call for help—his principle has always been one of co-operation right from the beginning.

God made the earth unaided by man, but he invited man to be a steward of it on his behalf. Adam and Eve were created to walk and commune with him in Eden. Right from the start they were intended to rule the earth in conjunction with their Creator, so it was important for them to know his mind concerning his handiwork. They needed time to be with him, to meditate on the beauty around them, and to listen to him as perhaps he outlined his reasons for making them and the various forms of life around them.

We also need communion with him, and his help today. Our conversion was not only to save us from hell, it was to bring us close to God so that we can enter into the plan of the ages: to rule the entire creation with the one who brought it into being. The details of this basic plan are often imparted during times of communion with him, especially as we meditate on the Scriptures in which he so often bares his heart. God's plan is for us to rule with him, not only in heaven but here on earth too. The full extent of this rule will take place in the future when we have our new bodies and abilities, but some of it takes place here and now. The Holy Spirit waits to instruct us through our meditation on Scripture as to how God wants us to affect our nation and our neighbours, how to halt corruption, how to lead the lost to God, how to build the church.

We especially need the help of the Holy Spirit when we begin a new chapter in our spiritual lives, such as a new devotion to God's word. Many people feel as though all hell is literally let loose when they start meditating on the Bible. This doesn't actually happen, of course, because evil powers are created beings: they cannot know everything which takes place in our lives, and their power is limited. But we are certainly up against them to some degree, as well as our flesh and our time-tables, and it is in these three areas where our main problems lie.

Our timetables

Some routines are fixed, such as the starting and finishing times in our place of work, or our schedule of lessons and lectures at school or college. But have you ever sat down with God to examine the way in which you use the rest of the time available to you? There are 168 hours in every week, whether you live in Aylesbury or Australia, and none of us is tied to daily work for all those hours. 'I haven't got time' is a feeble excuse. When you have a real desire for something you can always find time.

My wife and I always found the time to be with one another before we were married. I was at one college on a hill, and my wife-to-be was at an all-girls' college up another hill over a mile away. I could get there in about nineteen minutes flat (I usually was flat by the time I had finished attempting the land speed record!). Her college was guarded by a matron with a ferocious expression, plus a man-hating dog and a high wall, but I always found the time and the strategy to get there. If we have a favourite TV programme, we find time to watch it; if we have a hobby, we find time to do it. Let us spread our routines before the Lord and ask him to edit them rigorously.

Our flesh

Our cowardly, whining flesh is perhaps our greatest enemy. It whines at the prospect of losing sleep by rising early to pray; it bleats at the mention of fasting; it hates the word sacrifice; it tries to insist that most of our time should be spent in indulging its whims and fancies. When God looks at some of his yawning, pyjama-clad, flabby, self-centred fighting forces, he certainly needs courage to press on with his plan to use us to build his kingdom, crush the devil, act as stewards of his creation, and inherit heaven! But he does have that courage, praise his name! In the light of this, let us treat our flesh as the thief that it really is, robbing us of part of our destiny which is to know the Lord and to finish his work.

But how can we deal with such a powerful enemy as our flesh? First, remember that the power of God is greater than that of our flesh, and that our flesh can be put to death. This involves our wills working in conjunction with the Holy Spirit, as inferred in Romans 8:13—'If by the Spirit you are putting to death the deeds of the body [the flesh], you will live.' Secondly, remember that your regeneration (new birth) freed your will from enslavement to sin so you could obey God: 'Though you were slaves of sin, you became obedient from the heart' (Rom 6:17). All which previously hindered man was abolished when Jesus cried in triumph, 'It is finished!'

Our minds

As we set out to meditate, we will soon discover another problem: our minds wander. Some are more prone to this than others, but most people find problems here. God helped me some years ago in this area. I was sitting in a church service all ready to worship the Lord, when a woman came and sat down in front of me. She was wearing a hat like a portable cherry orchard; every time she moved her head the orchard was activated, much to my distraction and irritation. My mind was all over the place, but then God caused me to reflect on the fact that she was, after all, my sister, so I thanked him for saving her. Then I saw that she had lovely hair, so I thanked him for inventing hair. Then God reminded me that under that hair was a head, and in that head was a mind, so I asked him to fill her mind with thoughts of him, and as I prayed this I found my own mind filled with such thoughts too, so we both worshipped God together.

God delights to help us face up to and overcome such problems, and he rejoices because he sees that, as we progress, this will enable him to entrust even bigger things to us.

Let me emphasize some important points here. First, recall and read again God's frequent promises to help us. However, he will not do it all—he expects co-operation from us too. Secondly, don't underestimate the value of doing things aloud—they register more strongly in the mind when we do so. Choose your location wisely, of course. Try reading aloud, memorizing aloud, thinking aloud, and praying aloud. If you are still distracted, take the thing which distracts you and talk to God about it aloud. Then get back to where you were, all the time trusting the Holy Spirit to be training and focusing your mind.

Thirdly, get to know, love and trust the Holy Spirit whom Jesus gave to his disciples to help them. Even before he went back to heaven, Jesus detected the apprehension of his disciples when they were wondering how on earth (literally) they were going to fulfil the tremendous work which he was entrusting to them. He responded with these wonderfully encouraging words: 'I will ask the Father, and He will give you another Helper [advocate and intercessor], that He may be with you forever. . . . He abides with you, and will be in you. . . . He will teach you all things, and bring to your remembrance all that I said to you' (Jn 14:16-17, 26). Jesus also promised us that God the Holy Spirit would 'guide you into all the truth. . . . Whatever He hears, He will speak; and He will disclose to you what is to come. He shall glorify Me; for He shall take of Mine, and shall disclose it to you' (Jn 16:13-14).

This Holy Spirit is not a thing, nor a 'divine blob', but a person. He is God in exactly the same way as the Father is God and the Son is God. He is the one who brooded over creation (Gen 1:2), and the one who empowered Sarah to conceive in old age. It was he who gave Samson his strength, envisioned the prophets, and wrote the Scriptures. In co-operation with the Father and the Son, he brought about the virgin birth, enabled Jesus to live a perfect life and die an awful death. He raised him up again, and now imparts the benefits of salvation to everyone who is born again, as he baptizes them into the body of Christ (1 Cor 12:13). He knows the mind of God (1 Cor 2:10-11), and desires to let us into its secrets (1 Cor 2:12). He envelops us in his power (Lk 24:49) so that Jesus' words in John 14:12—'The works I do shall you do also'—may be fulfilled. He is expert with all temperaments—Moses the melancholic, Peter the impetuous, Thomas the doubter—so it is no excuse to say that you cannot get into Bible meditation because your temperament isn't inclined that way. The Holy Spirit lives within you, whatever your make-up. When we cry for help, he is the one who responds, he will lead us, he will speak to us, he will glorify Jesus through us. What more do we want?

Learning together

God never intended us to be loners. The church is not a collection of individuals who all do their own thing; it is a body, an army, a flock. These figures of speech infer the need for cohesion and co-operation in all aspects of our life together, including Bible meditation. Scripture exhorts us to help each other: 'Through love serve one another' (Gal 5:13). One way of obeying this injunction is to help each other to meditate in groups.

For many years Denis Clark and Campbell McAlpine ran a Bible Meditation Course. When Campbell left it, I took his place with Denis and began to learn more about meditating in the word, while at the same time teaching it to the students. When Denis died some years ago, I carried on with the help of my wife, Peggy, and Richard and Shirley Harbour.

During the course we found group participation very helpful and stimulating. We would read a passage aloud together from several versions of the Bible, then form into groups, praying for guidance and understanding as we spent some time in quiet contemplation of it. The group leader would ask for some come-back from each person and they would pray there and then on the basis of it. Alternatively, we would all assemble together and share and pray as a whole company, bringing together all our different insights on the word. Another time we would take one verse and memorize it, then all the people would go away to a quiet place for meditation on that verse, then reform into groups and share what God had said to us through it. On still other occasions we would read a psalm and proceed to pray through it one after the other, thus linking prayer and meditation. Sometimes everyone would sit on the lawn, or go for a 'meditation-and-prayer' walk. The group situation not only taught us many different ways of meditating together, but also helped us to pray in an informed manner for one another.

Visions and pictures may be given to us by God during times of contemplation. In one Bible meditation group a man had a picture in his mind, but thought it too trivial to mention. When pressed he shared it. It was of a baby playing with a gold necklace which his mother had put round his neck. After pondering this for a while, someone in the group said, 'That's lovely! The chain is gold, so it refers to something precious—the results of our Bible meditation which enrich us so much.' At the moment we may feel we are only playing with this art, and that we do not really understand it, but in time we will realize how precious it is. If we press on we will grow spiritually, learning to value and enjoy the fruits of our Bible meditation as we are aided by the Holy Spirit, who may well illumine us through visions and pictures.

Using our imagination

God gave us the power of imagination, so it cannot be wrong to use it. It can run away with us, however, so it needs to be handled carefully. It is probably best to exercise it when meditating with others, because when we share our imaginations we can help each other to spot things which might cut across Scripture. Some groups use their imagination to picture themselves in the situations mentioned in Scripture, such as Jonah in the belly of the great fish. One person in our group, having pictured himself in this situation, decided to make his will—a simple but practical step. He also determined to be ready if he was ever confined to a prison of some sort. Another person put herself in Abraham's place at Moriah, and began to wonder whether her devotion and obedience to God was anything like his. She decided it was not, and repented of her worldliness and began to live a more sacrificial life. If we are truly steeped in Scripture, it is not dangerous to use the natural ability of imagination during times of meditating on God's word.

We do not need to be on a course to help one another; we can learn the things mentioned above in our churches or our homes. A group known to me met every week for a year, and at the end of it they were far more spiritually mature than before. Their intercessions closed the local sex-shop and the school of witchcraft. This underlines yet again the close link between Bible meditation and prayer: Bible meditation brings us personally closer to God, it makes us sensitive to his heart, and this enables us to pray with feeling, accuracy and success.

Pause and ponder

Bible meditation may be difficult, but God offers us the help of his Spirit and that of our brothers and sisters.

10

Grist for the Mill

Grist is corn, ground in the mill and producing bread to eat which is chewed by the mouthful. Let me encourage you to grind, eat and chew using the resource material in this chapter, which enlarges on some of the points outlined in chapter 8.

For the sake of clarity I have listed the material under the sub-headings of words, phrases, verses and themes: I am, of course, aware that this is an artificial separation. The word 'grace', for example, is rich in itself, but there are also whole phrases and verses devoted to it, and it appears as a theme running right through the Bible. The following suggestions are meant to whet your appetite and give you an idea of what can be done. There are dangers in doing things this way: it is possible to get things out of context, take only that which appeals to us, or make the system an end in itself. However, most things in the Christian life have risks attached. Some readers may prefer to meditate steadily and consecutively through a whole book rather than take things from here and there, and I mention this method in the next chapter.

Words

Single words hold a surprising amount of meaning, and can illumine whole passages of Scripture for us. The word 'believe', for example, means far more than the mental acceptance of something; it means to trust in, cling to, and rely on. It is a doing word, implying whole-hearted action as in true conversion. When we became Christians, we realized the truth of the Bible, responded to it, reached out to God for the new life he promised, trusted him to do what he promised, and began to adhere to every command he gave us—all facets of believing in God.

The word 'love' means far more than just a feeling. It includes friendship: when God says he loves us he means that he is our friend (Jn 15:13-14). Love includes sacrificial giving: 'God so loved . . . that He gave' (Jn 3:16). True love is unselfish: Jesus said, 'I do not seek my own will but that of Him who sent Me', and when the Father's will was to reach out to us in grace, he did it, despite the frightful cost to himself and his own Son. Love is totally faithful, as demonstrated by God when he assures us, 'I have loved you with an everlasting love' (Jer 31:3). True love is characterized by commitment; God has committed himself completely to us: 'Of His fulness we have all received . . .' (Jn 1:16).

Place names

Place names are often very significant in Scripture. 'Bethlehem' means 'house of bread'. In the book of Ruth, Naomi went away from the house of bread into the land of the enemy. Later on in the Old Testament, Micah prophesied that the Messiah would come from Bethlehem (Mic 5:2), and Jesus Christ declared, 'I am the bread of life' (Jn 6:35). Putting these findings together gives us a very helpful insight into a single word.

The names of God

In time past many Jews regarded the name of God as so sacred that it should never be spoken. There was not actually any need to go to this extreme, but as Christians we should remember that we can and do get overfamiliar with God so that our respect for him dwindles. There is a need for reverential fear coupled with loving confidence in our relationship with our Father. Meditating on his names can help us to keep this balance.

Jehovah Jireh (Gen 22:14)

'The Lord will see or provide.' Is there anything which God cannot see or anything which he cannot provide? It is easy to give mental assent to the truth that God is all-seeing and provides abundantly. However, meditating on the name Jehovah Jireh will help produce real faith in our heart. Pause just now and consider that he saw you in the womb and that his eyes have never left you since. He numbers the hairs on your head (Lk 12:7), keeps track of your conversation (Mal 3:16), notes all your needs (Phil 4:13), as well as keeping every star in his memory (Ps 147:4), noticing the death of every sparrow (Mt 10:29), and upholding all things by the word of his power (Heb 1:3). Has he ever lost sight of you? Has he ever left you starving? Ponder on all this, and draw closer to him in trust.

Jehovah Mekadishu (Ex 31:13)

'The Lord my sanctifier.' Sanctification means being set apart for God and being made clean and pure. But if I am righteous, you may object, why do I need to be made clean? We have to understand that our righteousness is based on Christ's perfect sacrifice on Calvary, whereby his sinlessness is imputed to us when we believe in him as our Saviour. Sanctification is the cleaning-up process which the Holy Spirit begins when he enters our heart. Although every bad habit does not drop off straightaway when we are born again, we do now have the power to rid ourselves of them if we co-operate with God the Holy Spirit. If I *will* be sanctified, he *will* sanctify me.

Jehovah Nissi (Ex 17:5)

'The Lord my banner or protection.' What a testimony! As Romans 8:31 says, 'If God is for us, who is against us?' When we get to heaven I believe we will see how many times God has protected us from danger which we were unaware of—no wonder we will worship him there. But why not worship him here and now? After all, we must know some of the occasions when he has kept us or provided our needs, and surely we are grateful.

Jehovah Rohi (Ps 23:1)

'The Lord my shepherd.' An Eastern shepherd leads his sheep to pasture, although he cannot make them graze in it. He protects them day and night, notices their injuries and heals them, names them and remembers their names, restrains them with his crook when obstinate, and loves them like children. Think about the implications of these few simple observations and be encouraged that God loves us and watches over us in the same way.

Jehovah Tsidkenu (Jer 23:6)

'The Lord my righteousness.' One day Israel will rejoice in this glorious truth, but we can do so now. In our prayer times we can praise God for his wonderful grace in giving us the very righteousness of his dear Son. In our witnessing we can tell the world how to abandon the filthy rags of self-righteousness and to take instead the perfect righteousness which Jesus died and rose again to make available to all who believe. If our friends say, 'I would love to come to the Lord, but I am not good enough,' we can and should tell them that Jesus is our righteousness and that he is willing to be theirs too.

There is an old hymn which says: 'Jesus Thy blood and righteousness my beauty are, my glorious dress. . . .

Bold shall I stand in that great day, for who aught to my charge shall lay? Fully absolved through these I am, from sin and fear, from guilt and shame.' Sing it while you meditate on your beauty as you stand before a holy God, beautiful because 'He has clothed [you] with garments of salvation, He has wrapped [you] with a robe of righteousness' (Is 61:10).

The titles of God

'The Shepherd and Overseer of [our] souls' (1 Pet 2:25, NIV).

The word used for overseer here is the same as that for bishop or elder. It is good to know the loving care of an earthly bishop or elder, but in Jesus we have an immortal bishop who 'always lives to make intercession for [us]' (Heb 7:25). Earthly elders are expected by God to 'watch over [our] souls, as those who will give an account' (Heb 13:17). In Jesus we have an elder who does not miss a breath we take!

'The Father of lights' (Jas 1:17)

'Sun and moon, bow down before Him, dwellers all in time and space' as the old hymn says. In some wonderful way the stars, planets and moons must honour their Creator. Although they are awesome and magnificent, they are not eternal but changing—the sun sets and the moon wanes—unlike God 'with whom there is no variation or shifting shadow'. How completely we can trust the God who declares, 'I, the Lord, do not change' (Mal 3:6).

Names of people in Scripture

Although not every single name in Scripture has a significant meaning, it is worth looking at some. The names of Jacob and his sons, for example, make an interesting meditation. (Gen 49:1-27). Ponder them also in the light of the shrewd and perceptive words of blessing given to their descendants by Moses (Deut 33).

Jacob means 'supplanter' or 'following after'.

Reuben means 'behold a son'. As the first-born it was hoped that he would be an outstanding son, but he failed under testing.

Simeon means 'hearing'. The violent anger of both Reuben and Simeon disqualified them: they heard but did not heed.

Levi means 'joined'. He joined up with his brother, Simeon—a bad alliance.

Judah means 'he shall be praised'. Despite failing he was exalted to rule over others and was praised by them. What grace! Note Genesis 49:10—could this refer to Jesus?

Zebulun means 'dwelling'.

Issachar means 'bringing hire' or 'reward'. A strong man with a serving spirit, no wonder he was rewarded.

Dan means 'judge'. A shrewd and able man, but dangerous.

Gad means 'seer', 'lot' or 'fortune'. He could spot and deal with enemies, and despoil them.

Asher means 'happy'. He was rich—and happy. Note the beautiful words spoken by Moses in Deuteronomy 33:24-25.

Naphtali means 'wrestling'. He was blessed by God and was a blessing to others. Note Genesis 49:21—'He gives beautiful words.' Did he wrestle in prayer, I wonder?

Joseph means 'increase' or 'Jehovah adds'. God's blessing made him rich, and he shared it: he is described as 'a fruitful bough by a spring; its branches run over a wall' (Gen 49:22).

Benjamin means 'son of right hand'. Jacob's comment that Benjamin was 'a ravenous wolf' (Gen 49:27) could give the impression that he was a destroyer. But whom did he destroy? Weren't they God's enemies?

Phrases

It is well worth studying whole phrases in the Bible. Take 'the eyes of the Lord', for example. Proverbs 15:3 says, 'The eyes of the Lord are in every place, watching the evil and the good.' Yet Habakkuk 1:13 says, 'Thou canst not look on wickedness.' How can God's eyes be everywhere if he cannot look on wickedness, for sin is all over the place? If we compare the preceding phrase in the same verse, 'Thine eyes are too pure to approve evil,' we see that not looking here means not condoning sin or leaving it unpunished. 2 Chronicles 16:9 says, 'For the eyes of the Lord move to and fro throughout the earth that He may strongly support those whose heart is completely His.' What a comfort to feel them on you at this moment! Song of Solomon 5:12 describes the eyes of the Son of God as 'like doves, beside streams of water, bathed in milk.'

Another phrase to ponder over is 'the arm of the Lord' (Is 53:1). In Exodus 6:6 God promised Israel: 'I will also redeem you with an outstretched arm.' Note the fact that God took the initiative—he stretched out to them. What grace! Isaiah 52:10 says, 'The Lord has bared His holy arm.' An Eastern scholar once told me that this is a reference to the custom of a warrior chief who, when riding against his enemies, would take the long flowing sleeves which denoted his rank, tie the ends in a knot behind his neck, and pull his arms down so that they were bared. This left him free to draw his sword which was the signal for battle. When we consider that it is God who is doing this, we are moved to praise him for his deliverance of Israel and his conquest of all our foes at Calvary. We are also reminded that we share in the victory Jesus gained on the cross—our arms are to be bared for warfare too.

God's arms are not only mighty but caring and supportive: 'Underneath are the everlasting arms' (Deut 33:27). If those arms are underneath us, we cannot possibly drop out, even in the moment of death. It is helpful to look at the references to God's hands, too. Talking of those who would believe in him, Jesus points out that 'no one shall snatch them out of My hand (Jn 10:28), and as if that was not enough he goes on to say, 'And no one is able to snatch them out of the Father's hand' (Jn 10:29). What security this gives us, and what a reply to the evil one when he tempts us to doubt.

The phrase which describes Jesus as 'full of grace and truth' (Jn 1:14) focuses on two great themes of Scripture which should be held in tension, and also focuses on the one who literally personifies them. Not only did Jesus show the grace of God to Men, but he was utterly uncompromising in his declaration of the whole truth and counsel of God. This is beautifully illustrated by his encounter with the woman taken in adultery: he did not condemn her, but he did say, 'Sin no more.' Jesus' life radiated the truth of Psalm 85:10—'Loving kindness and truth have met together; righteousness and peace have kissed each other.' Perhaps this was most supremely shown at Calvary. Meditate on the faithful love of Jesus towards us. In grace he saved us; he forgives, protects and provides for us, and yet at the same time he reproves and even punishes us so that we keep within the paths of righteousness and thus arrive at our proper, and eternal, destination.

Whole verses

Whole verses repay careful meditation, bearing in mind what I said earlier about the danger of taking them out of context. Don't just pick your favourite verses all the time; be adventurous and choose more difficult ones. Some verses will yield a great deal, within reason of course. Proverbs 30:33 says, 'Pressing the nose brings forth blood,' but I don't think it will bring forth any great meditations. But a verse such as Hebrews 10:12—'But He, having offered one sacrifice for sins for all time, sat down at the right hand of God'—will bring forth a great deal; it will deliver us from fear of drawing near to God. Many Christians hardly know the full extent of God's love for them, and so live impoverished lives. They feel that we must attain to near perfection before we can really spend much time in God's presence, implying that Calvary was barely sufficient to take away our sin, and that a kind of evangelical penance is necessary to make us totally acceptable and welcome there. A good verse to read alongside Hebrews 10:12 is Galatians 2:20—'The life which I now live in the flesh I live by faith in the Son of God, who loved me, and delivered Himself up for me.' Meditate on who the Son of God is: the creator, owner and upholder of all things; the one who knows and sees everything that happens everywhere; and the one before whom all heaven bows down. Then think of the fact that he is in love with *you*! Such a reflection will absorb you for a long time, banishing doubt and blessing you abundantly.

The more Bible verses we memorize the better. Some are especially packed with divine truth. Consider, for example, 1 Peter 1:2—'Chosen according to the fore-knowledge of God the Father, by the sanctifying work of the Spirit, that you may obey Jesus Christ and be sprinkled with His blood: May grace and peace be yours in fullest measure.' Meditating on this will enable us to glory in the truth that we were chosen as individuals to enjoy salvation, even though we need to respond our-selves as well. We can go on to ponder on the word 'Father', and all that it implies, think over the work of the Spirit as he makes us holy, and see afresh that the object in all this is that we should obey the Son. 'If you love Me, you will keep My commandments.' Rejoice in the sprinkling of his blood which both cleanses and sets us apart for him. How wonderful to see the whole Godhead active in our salvation! And lastly, from this verse, lay hold of his grace and peace in fullest measure, rejoicing in the sheer abundance of it.

Themes

Press on further to meditate on some of the great themes of the Bible, such as grace, forgiveness and mercy. Be careful to maintain a balance, and choose themes such as judgement, anger and punishment as well. It is rare to find anyone who has meditated on the terrors of hell, and not too many meditate on the horrors of Calvary either. Those who take time to do the former become soul-winners because they realize what they have been saved from and what their unsaved loved ones are heading for. Those who do the latter tend to love the Lord in a very deep and special way, and to worship him in spirit and reality.

All the themes mentioned above are connected with one another. It is most rewarding to trace the occurrence of each one right through the Scriptures. When you have done this, find a verse which sums up the theme to some extent, memorize it, then chew it over till it grips your heart, and then share it with someone you know.

Grace

Grace means unmerited favour, kindness and goodwill, expressing itself in spontaneous generosity. It is the attitude of God's heart towards us, causing him to bring us to new birth. Scripture speaks of 'this grace in which we stand; and we exult in hope of the glory of God' (Rom 5:2). It is this 'amazing grace' which inspired John Newton to write the hymn of the same name.

When you have thought about the basic meaning of the word 'grace', use your concordance to pick out some of the main verses which focus on it—and memorize them—such as 2 Corinthians 8:9—'You know the grace of our Lord Jesus Christ, that though he was rich, yet for your sake He became poor, that you through His poverty might become rich.' Ponder the phrase 'our Lord Jesus', and revel in the fact that he is *your* Jesus. Then chew over the phrase 'the grace of our Lord Jesus' for a while. You may well find a desire to trace the evidence for this grace in the history of God's people in the Scriptures, in which case you need to go back to reading and studying the word.

God's grace is seen right at the beginning in Eden. He could have obliterated Adam and Eve because of their deliberate sin, but he planned to save them and their descendants through the sacrifice of his Son. He could have wiped out the whole of mankind by the flood, but in his grace he saved a remnant to give man another chance. The prophet Hosea's life was a demonstration of God's grace. Even when his wife left him yet again, God told him to buy her back from the slave market, which Hosea did, thus vividly dramatizing the grace of God towards his unfaithful nation, Israel, one of whose titles was Jehovah's wife. After David sinned with Bathsheba, God could rightly have abandoned his covenant in which he had promised to retain David's kingly line, but through grace he kept his word.

God's grace is demonstrated supremely at Calvary, where Jesus gave all he had so that we could be redeemed. He could have come down from the cross if he had wanted to, but in his grace He stayed there so that you and I could be saved. Meditate on Ephesians 2:8—'By grace you have been saved through faith; and that not of yourselves, it is the gift of God.' The theme of God's amazing grace runs throughout the pages of Scripture. If we trace it, and ponder it, we will find ourselves worshipping the Lord all the more, and becoming more gracious ourselves.

Forgiveness

Forgiveness means 'to send away'. One scripture which will help us understand this aspect of the word is Isaiah 44:22—'I have wiped out your transgressions like a thick cloud.' When God forgives our sins he sends them right out of his memory. When we sin we incur a debt, but forgiveness has the effect of cancelling our debts. When we pray, 'Forgive us our debts' (Mt 6:12), God graciously forgives our sin and thus cancels our debt. The word 'forgiveness' also means 'to loose from': when God forgives us he frees us from the punishment incurred by our sin. As we meditate on this lovely theme and begin to rejoice in our forgiveness, we must be careful to consider the condition laid down in Matthew 6:15—'If you do not forgive men, then your Father will not forgive your transgressions.' This is an instance of our need to meditate on a theme throughout the whole word, considering all aspects of it, even though we may start with only parts of it.

God always forgives us when we truly repent, no matter what our sin and how miserably we have failed him and others. After the resurrection, the angel told the women who came to the tomb: 'Go, tell His disciples *and Peter . . .*' (Mk 16:7, my italics). Why was Peter singled out in this way? I think it was because the Lord wanted to reassure him of his grace and forgiveness towards the friend who failed him miserably in his most critical hour. In the light of this, we can lift up our heads and receive this same forgiveness, whatever our sin, and go on in the strength of this.

Mercy

Mercy means, among other things, the manifestation of pity, compassion and tenderheartedness. The Lord's mercy towards us is wholehearted: 'God, being rich in mercy, because of His great love with which He loved us, even when we were dead in our transgressions, made us alive together with Christ' (Eph 2:4-5). God could quite legitimately have left us dead, but because of his tenderhearted mercy, he reached out to us and saved us. Read and find out how many times God showed his mercy in Bible times. And remember that the very fact that you are alive to read those words indicates the mercy of God in preserving your life.

Anger

Not the most popular subject for meditation, but very worth while. Anger, or wrath, means 'burning indignation caused by offence'. When it is applied to God we should not conclude that 'burning' means he is in a temper, rather it indicates a constant, implacable opposition to sin in any form. It is the only attitude that a holy God can have towards sin. God's feelings are strong and cause him to do strong things, even chastening his children severely on occasions. But he only does so because he is a faithful Father, and cannot bear to see us ruin and hurt ourselves by persisting in sin.

Judgement

This word is subject to much misunderstanding. Many non-Christians take it to mean punishment by a censorious and vindictive God. But judgement actually means to distinguish, give an opinion, separate evidence, or weigh something critically. God's judgement is always most carefully considered and absolutely just. It does not always cause him to condemn, it sometimes makes him set free. Before Calvary, God condemned men after weighing the evidence against them (cf. Gen 6:12-13). This evidence was so clear and overwhelming that he could do nothing else. However, after Jesus offered the one sacrifice for sin for ever on our behalf, God's judgement was that if man availed himself of the offering then he would be considered righteous and set free, but if he did not he would remain in a state of condemnation: 'But he who does not obey the Son shall not see life, but the wrath of God abides on him' (Jn 3:36). Hebrews 9:27 says, 'It is appointed for men to die once, and after this comes judgement'. For the Christian this judgement will mean the eternal life won for us by the Lord Jesus Christ.

Eternity

Like anger and judgement, eternity is not a theme we often meditate on. But it repays thought—after all, eternity is what we are heading for. Jesus talked about the future far more than the present because he had a right perspective. His objective was not only to save man from hell, but to bring him into the realm of everlasting day. Our tendency is to dwell on the here and now. We are time-bound, but what is time? Perhaps a divine detour from eternity in order to save us and enable us to enter it with the Lord.

Those who often speak about heaven are likely to be called super-spiritual, or 'so heavenly-minded that they are no earthly use'. But Paul says that 'the mind set on the Spirit is life and peace' (Rom 8:6), and the Spirit says through Colossians 3:2—Set your mind on the things above, not on the things that are on the earth.' Meditating on the scriptures which speak of heaven will enable us to obey the plain commands of the Lord conerning our day-to-day human life on earth. Our time here is our training-ground for the life everlasting, and we must always keep uppermost that we should be laying up treasure there and preparing to rule.

I I

More Grist for the Mill

Although it is good to meditate on individual words, phrases, verses and themes, we do need to read through and study the whole Bible, otherwise we will get hooked on a few favourite passages and will therefore become unbalanced in our understanding of the word. Space does not permit a full study of all the books of the Bible here, but I offer a few snippets from several books. They are really appetizers only, unstructured and incomplete, but I hope they will enable you to embark on more in-depth meditation on your own.

Genesis

Chapter 3:15—the first reference to Calvary. 'Her seed' refers to Jesus; 'He shall bruise you on the head' refers to Jesus triumphantly treading down the devil and 'You shall bruise him on the heel' refers to the wounds which Jesus suffered at the cross (cf. Jn 19:30; 1 Jn 3:8).

Chapter 3:21—the first evidence of sacrifice. An animal's life is taken in order to cover, or atone for, man's sins (cf. Heb 9-10).

Exodus

Chapter 25:22—God meets us at the mercy seat (the same word as propitiation) (cf. 1 Jn 4:10; Heb 4:16).
Chapter 34:6-7—our God is balanced and complete in all his ways. Enjoy his love but beware of his anger. Study the much-neglected but important doctrine of the anger of God.

Leviticus

This entire book speaks of the nature and cost of sacrifice and the danger of neglecting it. It reveals much about the holiness of God and the necessity for priestly mediators. It has more typical pictures of Jesus than any other book, and it is the key to the New Testament book of Hebrews.

Numbers

Chapter 11:1—God detests grumblers; they forget what he has done for them.

Chapters 13:30 and 14:24—God loves wholehearted men like Caleb, and he rewards them (cf. Rev 2:7, 11, 17, 26).

Deuteronomy

Chapter 4:20—do not tamper with God's word (cf. Rev 22:19). 4:24—God has a holy jealousy over us, and therefore requires obedience to his covenant. 4:31—in his compassion, God is faithful and merciful.
Chapter 6:7—parents, teach your children the word of God well. But don't just teach the letter of the law, teach the spirit of it too.
Chapter 28:1—every promise is conditional.

Joshua

Chapter 1:7-9—'Be strong. . . . Be careful to do according to all the law. . . . Meditate . . . on it day and night . . . then you will have success. . . . God is with you.' Why not chew this over for a week?

Chapter 7:11, 20-26—you could be the death of your family or friends. Sin in the camp (or church, or family) brings judgement (cf. 1 Cor 5:6-7; Acts 5:1-11). Remember that there is nothing vicious in God's judgement, he simply weighs all the facts and declares a verdict on the basis of them.

Chapter 14:6-15—meditate on Caleb, the wholehearted man of God. Be like him!

Judges

See how many times this phrase is repeated: 'They did not drive out the inhabitants [enemies].' Think of things you may not have driven out of your life.

Chapter 4—praise God for godly women. Make a study of Deborah.

Chapter 16:20—how tragic when the Spirit left Samson to his own devices. A born-again Christian has the Spirit of God within him always, but the Spirit can be grieved or frustrated, and in that sense his power is absent from our lives and testimony (cf. 1 Cor 10:12).

1 Samuel

Chapter 2:11–3:21—when priests become unfaithful, the word of God becomes rare; then sin grips a nation and it becomes corrupt. But God is never taken by surprise: he finds here a godly mother who freely gives her son to God, who then uses the boy to raise up the nation again. How gracious God is to reach out again and again (cf. Is 65:2; 2 Pet 3:9-13).

Chapter 5:1-5—the supreme power of God is shown over all the so-called gods of the heathens. (Dagon was the idol of an earthly cult, behind whom was an evil demon from the kingdom of darkness.) Don't forget to meditate on the fact that evil powers exist, the terrors of the pit, their eventual abode, and of course Christ's, and our, perfect victory over them.

2 Samuel

Chapter 11-12:20—consider the consequences of sin (cf.1 Chron 21:7 ff.). Do you want to make men and demons jeer at the sacred name of your loving Father?
Chapters 17-18—see what treachery does.
Chapter 23—let David's mighty men inspire you (cf. 2 Sam 15:14-15).

1 Kings

Solomon was immoral, disobedient, materialistic and a covenant-breaker. Find proof of this as you meditate through the book (see especially chapter 11).
Chapter 8:60—this verse gives a reason for the existence of the church today plus the admonition which will keep her successful if she obeys it.
Chapter 17 ff.—do not be overawed by Elijah, for he 'was a man with a nature like ours' (Jas 5:17), but be inspired by him to seek greater things from God.

2 Kings

Chapter 5:2-3—an insignificant girl, planted by God in the right place, changed a mighty man's life, and perhaps the nation (cf. Gen 37:28, 36; 41:40).

1 Chronicles

Look out for the meaning of names. Meditate through 1 and 2 Chronicles and note God's courageous dealings with a sinful nation, and also his dealings with David, who had weaknesses but was devoted to God.

Chapter 4:10—meditate on the prayer of Jabez. Is it good or bad?

Chapter 11:1,10—consider the sheer devotion of King David's mighty men, and their objectives. What a lesson for us!

Chapter 21:24—are our offerings costly or cheap?

We have already looked at these stories in 1 and 2 Kings, but meditate again on the differing accounts.

2 Chronicles

Chapter 7:11-22—God answers true prayer—with promises and warnings.

Chapter 15—Asa was a good man, but not drastic enough where sin was concerned. The 'high places' were centres of idol worship, and should have been destroyed. Have you got any idols or 'high places'?

Ezra

It is a costly (Ezra 2:69), dangerous (Ezra 3:3; 4:6-16) but joyful (Ezra 3:11) privilege to restore the house of the Lord. God's opponents are angry, but see how God causes the wrath of man to praise him (Ezra 6:6 ff.; cf. Ps 76:10).

Chapters 9-10—see the progression here. Sin is noticed; godly grief leads to prayer, fasting and confessions; this leads to repentance and drastic action, which then enables God to bless the nation.

Nehemiah

God put Nehemiah in a key place, gave him a burden to raise up the walls of Jerusalem, causing even an 'un-saved' king to help him, and used him to impart strategy and courage to the people, and to get them to work. God used Ezra to explain the law of God to those who had forgotten it, and he rejoiced to see his people turning to it in obedience again. Did they have Bible meditation courses I wonder (Neh 8:8)?

Nehemiah enquired about people (Neh 1:2), and prayed on the basis of it (Neh 1:4-11). He used the position God gave him to ask godly favours (Neh 2:5), and he inspired his fellows to work for God (Neh 2:18). Work, watch and pray—meditate on this admonition (Neh 4:9, 17).

Esther

Notice again how God puts people in key places for criti-cal occasions (Esther 4:14). God allowed Esther to be separated from her people, to be shut into a harem, pampered in a beauty salon, and to surrender herself to the king's enjoyment. However, God gave her favour with the people (Esther 2:15) and the king (Esther 2:17). This paved the way for the deliverance of the Jewish people (Esther 8:4). Meditate on the fact that God has a key place for all his people. Are you in it?

Job

God notices everything about his people. He knew Job's every action and every detail of his character. He was not afraid to boast of him to the angels ('sons of God') either (Job 1:6,8; cf. Heb 2:11—Jesus 'is not ashamed to call [us] brethren'). The story of God's dealings with Job does not make sense unless we see it from heaven's perspective. God is using his people as a demonstration for the sake of his angels—how else would they ever know what grace, for example, means? Meditate on this together with Ephesians 3:10.

Chapter 19:25-26—Job's words must have been music in God's ears. Does he hear a similar declaration from us?

Psalms

One doesn't know where to begin in suggesting suitable passages for meditation from such a vast collection. However, look at Psalm 1 and ponder the results of meditation. Learn more about stillness from Psalm 46: 10. Read Psalm 103: 12-14 and enjoy God's forgiveness, his fatherly sympathy, and his perfect understanding of our nature and weaknesses. Do a study on the Fatherhood of God—then chew it over for the rest of your life! To those whose prayers are long unanswered, press the prayer in Psalm 119:49.

Proverbs

Pearls of wisdom for those who read them.

Proverbs 3:12 reminds us of God's balanced love.

Proverbs 4:23 warns us to guard our heart, for important things come out of it.

Proverbs 7:3 says that God's word is so important that it must be engraved on our heart, i.e. memorized.

Proverbs 15:3 points out that God never misses a thing. If you do something good, he notices it; if bad, he sees it (cf. Ps 139:7-12).

Ecclesiastes

Practical wisdom for living, undergirded by inspired

truth.

Chapter 3:2-8 should be carefully considered.

Chapter 3:11—everyone is destined for eternity, spending it in either heaven or hades.

Chapter 4:9-12—the joys and strengths of partnership.

Chapter 9:10—make use of opportunity, for it does not last long.

Chapter 11:14—don't be over-cautious. What we need is faith.

The Song of Solomon

See chapter 12.

Isaiah

Chapter 1:18—how gracious God is to reason with men, and how perfect is his forgiveness. If we confess sin, and he forgives it, where is it?

Chapter 6:1-7—your prayer room is like this.

Chapter 9:6—this meditation will take you some while to digest, but persevere and you will know God better.

Chapter 11:1-5—this is the Spirit who dwells in you.

Chapter 21:6-12—God is looking for watchers; will you rise to his challenge?

Chapter 41:8—Abraham was God's friend (cf. Jn 15:14–15). 41:7—God rewards the desperate. 41:21—we can 'argue' with God. Prayer should be reasoned, not a shopping-list.

Chapter 42—what a revelation of God the servant; what an incentive to be like him.

Chapter 53—a prophetic description of Calvary (cf. Ps 22). Meditate on the horrors and the triumph of Calvary— it will make you truly grateful, and spur you on in your evangelism.

Chapter 61—if we obediently follow Jesus, our ministry

can be as powerful as his.

Jeremiah

Chapter 1:5—Jeremiah's birth was not an accident, and neither was yours. 1:6-7—neither false modesty nor unbelief have any place in the purposes of God (cf. 1 Tim 4:12).

Chapter 8:11—God is a heart surgeon: he does things thoroughly, going to the root of a matter. Listen out for 'first-aid' prophets, and avoid them.

Chapter 29:7,11,13—are you bothered about the welfare of your town or city? And would you like to know God's plans for you? If you earnestly seek him you will find him, and he will restore you.

Lamentations

Chapter 1:12—the heart-cry of an intercessor.

Chapter 3:22—if you feel that God has forgotten you, read this.

Chapter 5—a true intercessor identifies with those for whom he pleads.

Ezekiel

This is quite a hard book to get to grips with, and rather puzzling.

Chapter 1—plenty of material here for meditating on the majesty of God.

Chapter 3:1—this refers to what we are talking about in this book.

Chapter 22:30—God still searches for those who will 'stand in the gap'—the prayer gap, the evangelism gap, the priestly gap. Will you fill it?

Chapter 33:7-9—one of the most fearful responsibilities I

know; but what a privilege to warn our neighbours in God's name.

Chapter 36:25-27—God is speaking primarily to Israel, but this is applicable to the church too. In fact, it is the experience of the Christian. Does it make us grateful?

Daniel

Reading this book makes me glad that we have scholars, and that we will have good teaching in heaven and all eternity to listen.

Chapter 1:8—what a refreshing verse. God loves it when we do the same (cf. Ps 119:9-11).

Chapter 3:18—meditating on the faith and courage of these great men can urge us on to emulate them.

Chapter 4:34—to paraphrase Lord Denning's words about a very important person: 'Be you ever so high, the Lord is above you.' This was true of the mighty monarch Nebuchadnezzar: God humbled him and he was converted. Verses 34-35 are a great comfort to us if we feel intimidated by 'great' men.

Chapter 11:32—knowing God is not only a great privilege, it is the best way of establishing his kingdom (cf. Jn 5:19, 30).

Hosea

The most tender of all the prophets, Hosea was a man who knew the very heart of God through the 'fellowship of His sufferings' (Phil 3:10). When God required him to do an extremely difficult thing (Hos 1:2), he responded immediately (Hos 1:3). How long does it take me to obey?

Chapter 2—God lovingly corners his rebellious wife, Israel (symbolized here by Gomer), deprives her in his mercy, and leads her back to himself as she stops calling

him Baali (master) and again calls him Ishi (my husband). Meditate on God's wonderful promise in verse
19: 'I will betroth you to me forever.' He means *you*.
Chapter 5:10—woe to those who remove God's boun-
daries, i.e. his laws, as Britain has by legalizing homo-
sexuality etc., and as some sections of the church have by
denying the virgin birth. 5:15—God is capable of veiling
himself from his people, but only until they return.
Chapter 10:12—the time to seek God is now. Chew over
the 'doing' words in this verse, and remember that meditation must always lead to action.

Joel

Chapter 1:13-20—tactics for emergencies.
Chapter 2:12-17—God responds to such earnest repen-
tance. Many prophets spoke of God's judgement, as did
Joel, but notice the words of reassurance (Joel 2:18, 32).
A true prophecy, even though it is stern, will always
have undertones of love and overtones of grace.

Amos

Chapter 1:1—not all God's spokesmen were of noble
birth—Amos was a shepherd (cf. 1 Cor 1:27).
Chapter 3:3—the importance of harmony is stressed
here. Are you quarrelling with God or anyone else?
3:7—we can infer from this that prophets are just as
important today.
Chapter 5:15—'Hate evil, love good' (cf. Heb 1:9).
Chapter 8:11—in the light of this, let us step up our study
and meditation on the word. How will we cope without
our Bibles if we do not?

Obadiah

This book carries a warning to the high and mighty of this world, but the high and mighty in the church should heed it too (Obad 14). God's perfect justice is foretold in verse 15. Don't miss the thrill of the last line in the book.

Jonah

Chapter 1:1-3—compare this with Luke 9:62. The rest of the chapter shows that God has courage enough to be very firm when his servants disobey him.

Chapter 2:7—a good remedy for spiritual fainting-fits. 2:10—God has absolute and supreme power over everything. All creation hears his voice and obeys. The rest of the book shows how great is God's compassion, even on those who are his enemies (see Jon 3:10; 4:11).

Micah

Chapter 1—God hates rebellion and he will deal with it, especially in his people. Do we lament over it in the spirit described in verse 8?

Chapter 3:11—leaders can be corrupt and deluded. How much do I pray for the leaders in my church—and my nation?

Chapter 4:3—wars cease when Jesus is king.

Chapter 5:2—God uses insignificant things, and people, for great things.

Chapter 6:8—God's pattern for our life.

Chapter 7:18—God never harbours grudges.

Nahum

Chapter 1—God is no softie, but there is good news (Nahum 1:15).

Chapter 2:1-2—we need to be watchful, but think of the one who is with us.
Chapter 3:8—learn from history.

Habakkuk

Chapter 1:2—does this sound familiar? Follow Habakkuk's example and wait on and for the Lord—it always pays to do so. God does not overlook the world's sin (Hab 1:13). Finite minds cannot cope with complete revelation; mystery is merciful (Hab 1:5).
Chapter 3:2—this is the kind of prayer God listens to, and the reaction he loves (Hab 3:16-19).

Zephaniah

Chapter 1:5—astrology is clearly idol worship. 1:12—laziness and apathy offend God.
Chapter 3:17—God exults over *you* (say your name) with shouts of joy. (RSV: 'He will exult over you with loud singing.')

Haggai

Chapter 1:4—which matters most to you, God's affairs or yours (cf. Mt 6:33)? 1:10-13—a right response to God's word brings a response from him.
Chapter 2:8—who really owns the world's wealth? If short, consult the owner.

Zechariah

Chapter 1:8-14—meditate on the ministry of angels; they patrol the earth and serve the church (cf. Zech 6:1-7; Heb 1:4).
Chapter 2:8—this refers to Israel and the church.

Chapter 3:2—the safest way to rebuke the Enemy.
Chapters 7:9 and 8:17—behaviour God loves.
Chapter 14:1-9—he will come, and we will be with him.

Malachi

Chapter 1:6—true children reverence their father—and God is our Father. 1:13—it is an insult to regard God's service as tiresome.
Chapter 2:6-7—the hallmarks of a true priest. 2:16—marriage is for life. Have you reviewed your marriage vows recently?
Chapter 3:16—God loves a good book!

Matthew

Chapter 1—don't groan over genealogies, investigate them.
Chapter 2:15—'That which was spoken through . . . the prophet might be fulfilled.' Find at least twelve occurrences of this phrase in Matthew's gospel.
Chapter 5—what do the Beatitudes say to you?
Chapter 20:22—think before you speak!
Chapter 26:40—let the Lord's disappointment urge us on to a more disciplined prayer life.

Mark

Chapter 1:3—preparing God's way is our task and privilege too. But how do we go about it? 1:22—consider the authority of Jesus mentioned in this verse in the light of his actions described in chapter 1:23, 34, 39 and chapter 2:10-11. He gives this same authority to us (Mk 3:14).
Chapter 3:25—division is the devil's weapon.
Chapter 4:24-32—God always responds to faith.
Chapter 5:43—Jesus shunned publicity; the church loves

it (cf. Mk 1:34, 45; 2:1; 3:7, 12; 4:35-36; 5:43; 7:24,36; 8:2630).

Luke

Jesus can help in every temptation (cf. 1 Cor 10:13; Heb 2:18). Look out in this book for occasions when Jesus cared for and helped very different people, especially women (e.g. Mary, Elizabeth, Peter's mother-in-law, the widow at Nain, the woman with a haemorrhage, Jairus' daughter, the woman with a spirit of infirmity, and the importunate widow). Men were also loved and helped (e.g. the ten lepers, Pharisees, publicans, a rich ruler, a blind man, and Zacchaeus).

John

Chapter 1:1—Jesus, the Word of God, is the expression of what the Father wanted man to know about himself.
Chapter 2:5—the gospel according to Mary.
Chapter 4:34—the consuming passion of Jesus' life. It should be ours too.
Chapter 5:19, 30—note the sheer economy of Jesus' life and ministry.
Chapter 12:42—secret disciples are not disciples.
Chapter 14:2—Jesus is personally preparing our home in heaven. 14:15—the acid test of love.
Chapter 16:9—the ultimate sin is not believing in the Son of God.

Acts

Chapter 1:4—study the promise of the Father (cf. 2:33; 5:32).
Chapter 3:6—what I have I share: this should be, and can be, our testimony.

Chapter 5:11—this kind of fear keeps the church healthy. 5:32—the Spirit is not comfortable with the disobedient.

Chapter 15:38—even apostles are fallible. What a comfort!

Chapter 23:11—our times are in God's hands (cf. Ps 31:15).

Romans

Chapter 1:24—a nation cannot trifle with God and get away with it (cf. Gal 6:7-8); every Christian should pray for the nation.

Chapter 6:14—victory is possible, for God has said so.

Chapter 8:31-39—what more can God say?

Chapter 12:1-2—God's powerful plea. Who will respond?

Chapter 14:12—get ready now, then we won't blush up there!

1 Corinthians

Chapter 2:12—the Spirit loves to show us what is in the heart of God.

Chapter 6:13—is God comfortable in the temple of my body?

Chapter 11:27-30—carelessness costs lives.

Chapter 14:1—gifts are not given to the faint-hearted.

Chapter 15—ponder over our glorious hope of resurrection.

2 Corinthians

Chapter 1: 3-6—let God comfort you now.

Chapter 3:18—we will all be like the Son of God.

Chapter 5:10—tremble if you are holding on to sin; rejoice if you have laid up treasure to receive at this throne. 5:21—for me this is the most glorious, but baffling, verse in Scripture.

Chapter 10:4-6—these weapons are mighty, but only if they are used.

Chapter 13:11—this is normal Christianity.

Galatians

Chapter 2:6—God has no favourites. 2:20—discuss this in your group, and receive a blessing from it.

Chapter 4:7—slave, son, heir: what a progression! But some sons still live like slaves.

Chapter 5:1—the secret of continual freedom.

Chapter 6:1—sound advice on how to deal with those who have fallen into serious sin.

Ephesians

Chapter 1:7—God does not forgive grudgingly.

Chapter 3:10—we are demonstration models for God; he teaches angels through us. 3:20—don't insult a great God with small prayers.

Chapter 4:15—God's norm for the tongue.

Chapter 5:1—like Father, like child. How does your life measure up against this?

Chapter 6:12—all Christians should be at war.

Philippians

Chapter 1:6—God does not give up on us. 1:21—if our meditation on the Lord is constant, this is likely to be our testimony. 1:27—the plumb-line for our lives.

Chapter 2:1-8—when God tests us, it is to help us to see how close we are to the glorious example of his Son.

Chapter 3:10—our earnest desire, surely?

Chapter 4:6—anxiety destroys; peace preserves.

Colossians

Locate all the 'in him' and 'through him' phrases in this book, and then mull over their implications for your Christian life.
Chapter 3:1—we are supposed to be heavenly minded.
3:8-10—only we can 'put off' and 'put on'. It takes the positive action of our will, and although God never forces our will, he responds in help the moment we exert it.
Chapter 3:18-21—the family, God's building-block for society.
Chapter 3:22; 4:6—God's order for society.

1 Thessalonians

Chapter 1:4—God chose us—and that is gloriously that!
Chapter 2:4—we have been entrusted with the gospel; may we be good stewards of it.
Chapter 4:1—as we walk in accordance to biblical principles, and thereby please God, let us aim to excel still more. 4:13-18—meditate on this constantly; revel in it; get ready for it.
Chapter 5:24—what an encouragement!

2 Thessalonians

Chapter 2:2—those who are well grounded in Scripture will not be easily shaken. 2:11—if men want delusion, God will simply confirm their choice. This is not vindictive, but fair.
Chapter 3:13—keep going: rewards await us, God is with us, and it is worth doing good.

1 Timothy

Chapter 1:4—this is a warning for us today not to run after Christian novelties or adulate the 'in' speaker. We must not become 'News of the World' Christians!

Chapter 2:4—the earnest desire of God, and the one who linked him with man (1 Tim 2:5).

Chapter 3:1-13—such high standards for leadership should make us tremble. How much, then, do leaders need our prayers.

Chapter 4:13—a much-neglected blessing. Try it in church—and in the market!

Chapter 5—honour those who are older (think of all those who have blessed you). 5:14—frustrate the evil one. 5:21—meditate on partiality, and see if you are guilty.

Chapter 6:17—God is never a miser.

2 Timothy

Chapter 2—soldiers, athletes, farmers, workmen, vessels, servants: all good meditations.

Chapter 3:1—God clearly warns us, therefore, don't moan, just overcome.

Chapter 4:8—no cross, no crown.

Titus

Chapter 1:2—God cannot lie; meditate on his promises in Scripture.

Chapter 2:2-3—older men and women have essential ministries—no redundancy in the kingdom! 2:14—one great reason for salvation.

Chapter 3:9—if Christians did this, there would be more time for evangelism.

Philemon

Chapter 1:2—our homes can be so useful to God. 1:7—a ministry which is open to all. 1:11—God is in the transformation business.

Hebrews

Chapter 1—feast your eyes on God the Son, this chapter is full of him.

Chapter 2:6-8—catch a glimpse of your position and future. 2:15—there is a remedy for fear. 2:18—cf. 1 Cor 10:13.

Chapter 3:13—we need the help of our fellow believers to prevent the horror referred to in verse 19.

Chapter 4:16—this is our refuge, let's live there.

Chapter 5:8—how profitable suffering is.

Chapter 6:10—God loves to encourage us. Enjoy this verse.

Chapter 7:25—when you feel dry and hopeless and prayer languishes, read this.

Chapter 9:12—when doubts of salvation come, read this statement about our *eternal* redemption.

Chapter 10:23—another fact to beat the devil with.

Chapter 11—take each character, study it, chew it over, and aim to follow his or her example.

Chapter 12:5-13—what a faithful Father we have. Respond to him.

Chapter 13:14—we are exiles; let's make sure our lives prove it.

James

Chapter 1:2—a gloriously irritating verse. 1:8—God uses the single minded. 1:22—words are cheap; obedience is what really counts.

Chapter 2:9—snobbery and favouritism are obnoxious to God; he knows nothing of 'class'.
Chapter 3:3-12—some facts about our murder weapon—but God can change it into a scalpel.
Chapter 4:7-8—there are conditions for victory. 4:14—life is brief, so let's get on with the job.
Chapter 5:9—please be careful—you may be judged. 5:17—don't just admire these men, emulate them.

1 Peter

Chapter 1:3-9—with an inheritance like this, surely we can put up with trials? 1:13-25—this is a powerful plea for realism.
Chapter 2:5, 9—we are priests—and priests meditate, pray and plead in the presence of God. 2:23—how do we react to such treatment?
Chapter 3:1—submission is not subjugation; headship brings responsibility.
Chapter 4:8—love 'overlooks' a multitude of sins. Try it.
Chapter 5:6—promotion comes from God, but only to the humble.

2 Peter

Chapter 1:11—a careful, obedient Christian walks tall in heaven.
Chapter 2:9—another comforting verse.
Chapter 3—don't be surprised when the world mocks us, it always has done, but get ready for the great day.

1 John

Chapter 1:3—'Our fellowship is with the Father, and with His Son.' What have you shared with them today? 1:9—what relief this verse gives.

Chapter 2:3-11—strong warnings against hypocrisy. 2:15—the world is a flirt and a seducer. Our faithfulness to God is our protection.
Chapter 3:3—our Christian hope should lead to practical Christian living.
Chapter 3:8—what a victory! It's part of our responsibility to enforce it here and now.
Chapter 4:1—we live in an era of delusion, therefore we must test everything and covet the gift of the discerning of spirits.
Chapter 5:15—the key to answered prayer.

2 John

Verse 4—God loves to see us doing the same.
Verse 6—love is shown practically as well as communicated emotionally.
Verse 8—the conditions for a full reward.

3 John

Verse 2—John desires us to be whole people. Spiritual health is linked with physical well-being.
Verses 5-8—faithful workers need faithful supporters.
Verses 9-10—unfortunately we have such men around today.
Verse 12—but thank God we have some like Demetrius.

Jude

Verse 1—meditate on the words 'called', 'beloved', and 'kept'.
Verse 3—never have we needed to contend more earnestly for the faith. But the faint-hearted will never do it.
Verses 14-15—justice will prevail when Jesus comes again. Meditate on other scriptures which speak of

justice.

Verse 24—God guarantees to glorify us.

Revelation

Chapter 1:12-20—another glorious vision of our Lord. Feast on it.

Chapters 2 and 3—love-letters from Jesus to his bride. How loving and utterly faithful.

Chapter 4—a glimpse into our future home, and of the one with whom we will live for ever.

Chapter 5:5-6—meditate on Jesus as the lion and the lamb. Find other verses which enlarge on this. 5:9-14—this is what worship is like in heaven. Do you ever bow down in your church?

Chapter 6:9-11—Christians who have passed away are conscious now.

Chapter 7:15—we are not inactive in heaven.

Chapters 8-10—God judges the world, and we will be with him when he does it.

Chapter 12:10—meditate on the whole question of authority. God has total authority, and he gives it to us (cf. Lk 10:19).

Chapter 14:1—connect this with other scriptures, such as Zechariah 14:4 and Jude 14.

Chapter 17:14—rejoice in the Lord, and in the position he has given us.

Chapter 19—the church is described as a bondservant, a bride and an army: all these concepts are worth thinking over.

Chapter 20—the finale of the ages.

Chapter 21—heaven, our home for ever. Get to know it by meditation, for it will urge you on to finish the work on earth and get there.

Chapter 22:12—there are rewards in heaven. Look forward to them. 22:18—those who say that the age of miracles is over should ponder this verse. Those who say the same about the gifts of the Spirit should do likewise.

I want to repeat what I said at the beginning of these two chapters on grist for the mill, namely, that these are only bits and pieces from the Bible, and certainly not a commentary. But what glorious bits, and what super pieces! I hope they enthuse you, urge you on, bless you, build you up, and encourage you to dig deep into the Bible. Then you will be well able to serve God on the earth, and will not be ashamed when you have to appear before the judgement seat of Christ.

Pause and ponder

With such a harvest to gather from, there is no excuse for failure to reap.

12

King Solomon's Mines

This chapter is an example of how to meditate on one book of the Bible, virtually verse by verse, as opposed to meditating on selected portions of it as part of a study of an individual word or an overall theme. It could serve as a series of daily meditations, although it is purposely far from complete and should not therefore be treated as a studied commentary.

Many regard the Song of Solomon strictly as allegory, or a semi-canonical book, or even one which is too embarrassing to read in public. Others regard it as a kind of biblical sex manual, while still others say that it is not a doctrinal book and therefore we should not take teaching from it. It is certainly not an easy book to interpret, and there are dangers in trying, but that is true of many others parts of the word. I suspect that many avoid preaching from it because they do not have a sufficient grasp of the overwhelming and intimate love of God for his people, therefore they find they cannot get to grips with it.

There is no space here for a full commentary on the Song of Solomon, so I will simply sketch a background to it and pick out some of the highlights as I see them. My interpretation will no doubt be regarded as too devotional by some, suspect by others, and fanciful to a few. I hope more than anything else that it will help some to be more deeply in love with God, and therefore more obedient to his commandments.

Solomon's Song is a love story, and there are three main characters: King Solomon, the shepherd, and the Shulammite woman. King Solomon cannot be a picture of Jesus, as some have said, because he was worldly, materialistic and disobedient to the law of God. He made slaves of his fellows, and married heathen women and worshipped their gods. Therefore I suggest that he is a picture of the world and its temptations. The shepherd does not seem to be so much in evidence for he is out on the hills tending his sheep, but he keeps a loving eye on the woman to keep her safe, for he loves her deeply (Song 2:9). This seems to make him, rather than King Solomon, a good picture of Jesus. In John 10:11 Jesus says, 'I am the good shepherd.' He is not visible in the world at the moment, for he is busy preparing a glorious fold (Jn 14:2), but he has promised that he will come for his bride in glory (Mt 24:30-31).

The woman seems to be a very lovely picture of the Christian. She is a bride, and Christians are called the bride of Christ (Rev 21:9). She had probably been captured by the king's talent scouts and brought to the harem because of her beauty. The king did everything in his power to persuade her to marry him, or at least be his concubine, but she firmly refused because she was in love with the shepherd and she was utterly loyal to him despite the king's blandishments. The other women in the harem are amazed at her temerity in turning down the king's proposal; they cannot understand how she could possibly prefer another man to the king. They seem to be a picture of those around us, described in

Scripture as 'natural' (cf. 1 Cor 2:14—'A natural man does not accept the things of the spirit of God . . . because they are spiritually appraised.') The shepherd and the woman both look forward to a day when they will be together, away from all the sin and hypocrisy of the palace. And the bride of Christ would echo, 'Amen. Come, Lord Jesus' (Rev 22:20).

The main themes

The strong love between bride and groom, i.e. the Shulammite woman and the shepherd (Song 2:16; 7:10).

His utter faithfulness and her relative faithfulness (Song 5:2-6).

His jealous, loving anger (Song 5:6).

The seduction of the world and the flesh (cf. 1 Jn 2:15–17, Amplified Bible).

The dangers of the unequal yoke. Supposing she had married the king! (cf. 2 Cor 6:14.)

No need for inhibitions. What is wrong with speaking of sexual union in a pure context? The Bible is frank and wholesome.

Gems from the mine

In this section I will assume that we are the woman/bride and that Jesus is the shepherd/bridegroom. This makes for simpler interpretation. I have used scriptures from elsewhere in the Bible to help draw out the truth expressed in the poetry of the Song of Solomon. The NASB margin gives the best indication of who is talking to whom. The following are only brief jottings or seed thoughts, meant to get you started on this book.

Chapter 1:2

Our deep longing for the expressions of Jesus' love. We need to make ourselves beautiful for him by holiness and spiritual virtue.

Chapter 1:3

Everything about Jesus is fragrant (cf. Ps 45:8). Consider the sheer fragrance of his name (cf. Eph 5:2), then ponder the fragrance we can bring to him (Jn 12:3).

Chapter 1:4

The world's longing for satisfaction, expressed here in the cry of the harem women. We are the ones who have been chosen for the royal chamber (cf. Jn 6:44; 12:32; 14:2-3). Is our desire to follow him into it? (cf. Ps 63:1; 84:1-2). How wonderful that we benefit from his initiative. Both bride and groom say, 'Let us run together!'

Chapter 1:5-6

We are different from the world, as the Shulammite woman is different from the harem women. Those in the world are in darkness and are corrupt, but Jesus describes us as 'the salt of the earth [and] the light of the world' (Mt 5:1314). Again, in John 17:16, he describes his disciples as 'not of the world'. Paul warns against being conformed to this world in Romans 12:2.

Chapter 1:7

Our great longing should be to be with him, doing his work, in the same way as two lovers always want to be with one another. Indeed, our beloved warned: 'No one can serve two masters' (Mt 6:24). If we love God, there is no problem as to who is master. In any case, as Peter said when Jesus asked if his disciples would also leave him, 'Lord, to whom shall we go? You have words of eternal life' (Jn 6:68). If God has given us the privilege of 'working together with him' (2 Cor 6:1), then that is what we should long to do.

Chapter 1:12

Closeness to Jesus brings forth our worship. A glimpse of God excites us, his beauty enthrals us, his majesty awes us, and his love satisfies us. God enjoys our closeness too (cf. Ps 45:9-15).

Chapter 2:1

'I am the rose of Sharon,' we say, 'the lily of the valleys.'
There were millions of roses, or crocuses, on the plain of
Sharon, so what is so special about us? But the Lord
declares that 'like a lily among the thorns, so is my dar-
ling among the maidens'.

Chapter 2:3

We respond to his declaration of love with tender words
concerning him. We are delightfully secure in him, for in
his shadow there is rest, safety and enjoyment (cf. Ps
91).

Chapter 2:4

He has brought us to the most honoured place. The
banner, or canopy, was a sign of power and splendour,
and it was the highest honour for a noble to invite one to
sit under it with him.

Chapter 2:5-6

The love between us and the Lord is of the most intimate
and powerful kind (cf. Ps 63; Jn 17:21-26).

Chapter 2:8

He is coming! (cf. 1 Thess 4:16; 2 Pet 3:12; Rev 10:6).

Chapter 2:9

He watches to see if we are faithful (Lk 18:8).

Chapter 2:10

The bridegroom is the one who decides when it is time to
go (1 Thess 4:13).

Chapter 2:14

He desires close and private fellowship with us. Do we
satisfy his desire? (cf. Jn 4:23).

Chapter 2:15

Let us deal ruthlessly with everything which spoils our
fellowship with God (cf. Heb 12:1).

Chapter 2:16

How wonderful! The Lord is mine simply because he
wants to be (Jn 15:9; 2 Cor 6:18; Col 1:22). And he is

also mine because I made him mine (Jn 1:12). I am his through creation (Ezek 18:4), redemption (Tit 2:14; 1 Pet 1:18), and through his choice of me (Jn 15:16).

Chapter 3:1-4

For the one who is deeply in love with the Lord, there is nothing more terrible than to lose the sense of his presence. Although this may be the result of our persistence in some sin, it may also be a time of testing ordained by God to lead us into greater maturity.

Chapter 4:1-15

Our Lord wonders of us in the most deep and tender way, appreciating all that is lovely in us. Many Christians are unable to accept his approval because they suffer from a spiritual inferiority complex in which they believe that there is nothing good in them. But this grieves and insults the Holy Spirit who dwells within us and sanctifies us.

Note especially verse 7: can the Lord really say there is no blemish in us? Look at Isaiah 61:10—'I will rejoice greatly in the Lord . . . for he has clothed me with garments of salvation, he has wrapped me with a robe of righteousness.' We are called, justified, and glorified (Rom 8:29-30; 1 Cor 6:11). We are in Christ, spotless and radiantly beautiful like him. When God looks on us, he sees us 'in Christ'.

Turn to Colossians and read through it, culling the 'in Christ' statements. It will make your mind boggle (boggle on, O mind, I love it).

Chapter 4:8-9

Respond to his loving invitation: 'Come with me' (cf. Ps 23:2-4—'He makes me lie down in green pastures; he leads me beside quiet waters. . . . He guides me into the paths of righteousness . . . [and] through the valley of the shadow of death.') Wherever we may be, we are safe with him.

Note especially verse 9. This truth is so staggering that

it took me months to believe it! We have captured the heart of Jesus, the Son of God! Many Christians will immediately respond to this, 'It's a lovely thought, and I wish it was true of me, but of course I will never be worthy enough for that.' To think like this is an absolute insult to God, and it verges on a rejection of the gospel itself. The scriptures cited in the previous paragraph are proof enough of the truth of verse 9, but I offer a few more from both the Old and New Testaments: Ps 18:19; Is 49:15; 62:5; Jer 31:3; Hos 11:8; Jn 3:16; 15:13; 17:23; Rom 5:8; 8:35-39; Eph 3:19. If you grasp this truth and it grasps you, it will transform your life.

Chapter 4:12-15

This is a beautiful picture of what our hearts and lives can be if we truly love the Lord. We are a garden locked up, only for him (cf. Rom 12:1-2); a refreshing spring, sealed for him (cf. Jn 4:14). We are fruitful (cf. Mt 3:8; Gal 5:22; Col 1:10); fragrant (cf. 2 Cor 2:15; Eph 5:2; 1 Pet 2:20-33. Myrrh and aloes were used in embalming oils, and are thus connected with suffering. The way we react to suffering can be fragrant to God). Are we like the bride in verse 16 who welcomed the cold north wind of adversity to come and blow on her garden so that its fragrance would come to the nostrils of the one she loved?

Chapter 5:1

If Jesus is invited to come into the garden of our heart, he always does so, because he always wants to. How gracious of him to make it possible for us to give him pleasure.

Chapter 5:2-8

How fickle the woman is. After such a wonderful time with her lover, she fails to respond to him when he asks her for a little sacrifice. He was a shepherd, working day and night (cf. Jn 5:17). She was too tired to dress and open the door to him, yet he knocks again (cf. Rev 3:20).

How patient he is, and how gracious (cf. Is 65:2). His love for her is so great, and he desires her good so much, that he teaches her a lesson—when she does condescend to open her door, he has gone (cf. Hos 5:15). If you have ever known the utter desolation of losing the sense of God's presence, then you will sympathize with the woman's feeling that there does not seem to be anything left to live for. She searches the streets, desperately seeking him. She asks the women of Jerusalem that if they find her lover to tell him she is lovesick. But, they say, what is so special about him? How will they be able to detect him from among all the other men? She then tells them, with glowing face and in ardent language, what her beloved is like.

Chapter 5:10-16

To me this is one of the most glorious descriptions of Jesus in the Bible. We should test it against other parts of the word, and while we must not let our imagination run away with us, let's not be too unadventurous.

Chapter 5:9-16

The reality of the woman's rekindled love causes others to enquire about her beloved. This is the essence of a genuine and effective testimony (cf. Acts 4:13—'They . . . began to recognize them as having been with Jesus).

Chapter 5:10

If her lover was only 'dazzling', she would be afraid of him (cf. Is 6). But he is dazzling *and* ruddy. Applying this to Jesus, we could say that if we only saw his holiness we would never dare come near him, but he was ruddy too, and he had the colour of a man (cf. Jn 1:14). If Jesus is really outstanding above all to us, then he will be pre-eminent in our lives.

Chapter 5:11

Gold is a picture of deity, and thick black hair to an Eastern woman was a sign of strength, handsomeness and virility. The divine nature and true strength and manliness were seen in the Son of God.

Chapter 5:12

The eyes of the Lord make a tremendous subject for Bible meditation. Doves are gentle; God's eyes are gentle. Doves are clean; so is God. Doves are faithful; so is God.

Chapter 5:13

Does God really want to embrace us cheek to cheek and lips to lips? Many would not dare say yes, but we have no reason to be afraid. Hebrews 4:16 says, 'Let us therefore draw near with confidence to the throne of grace'—we can come close to the one who sits on the throne and who issued the invitation. Did God endure Calvary to bring us only within arm's length? His lips always speak that which is true and pure (lilies are a symbol of purity), and his words are fragrant like liquid myrrh, therefore we can trust him when he says he wants us near him. Ponder some of those words: 'Their sin will I remember no more' (Jer 31:34); 'I will never desert you, nor will I ever forsake you' (Deut 31:16); 'I go to prepare a place for you' (Jn 14:2).

Chapter 5:14

God's hands make an enlightening subject for meditation. Using a concordance, compare other scriptures with this one.

Chapter 5:15

This verse, with its imagery of strength, solidity and grandeur, reminds us of the absolute stability of the Lord (cf. 'I, the Lord, do not change' (Mal 3:6); 'Jesus Christ is the same yesterday and today, yes and forever' (Heb 13:8); 'He will not be disheartened or crushed' (Is 42:4); 'Trust in the Lord forever, for in God the Lord, we have an everlasting Rock' (Is 26:4)).

Chapter 5:16

God is my beloved and God is my friend. Meditate on this truth until you believe it with all your heart. Remember, God longs to be our friend, but there is a condition: 'You are My friends, if you do what I command you' (Jn 15:14).

Chapter 6:1

Those who testify as the woman has done will have no problem in winning others to the Lord. Note that it was as she began to miss his immediate presence that she went into raptures about him. Are you conscious of his presence? Do you have a genuine testimony? Or are you selfish with the gospel, depriving your friends of its benefits?

The rest of the Song of Solomon reiterates much that we have already looked at, so my comments on chapters 6-8 will be quite brief. Ask God to show you personally what he wants you to understand from it.

Chapter 6:2-3

The woman rejoices over her lover's delight in her: she is the garden where he loves to go. Notice how she repeats the phrase: 'I am my beloved's and my beloved is mine.' As she meditates on this wonderful truth, she increasingly believes it, and is therefore encouraged and strengthened by it. We should follow her example. God is constantly telling us of his love for us; reflect on Isaiah 62:5 —'As the bridegroom rejoices over the bride, so your God will rejoice over you.'

Chapter 6:4-7:9a

The shepherd responds to her invitation and comes to receive from her and enjoy her. He notes her beauty in appreciative detail and speaks freely of it to others, being quite unashamed of his love for her. There is nothing to be ashamed of in womanly beauty. God went to great lengths to make woman attractive to man and vice versa. Seeing physical beauty from God's point of view makes the relationship between the opposite sexes pure, sacred and enjoyable.

Jesus does not fail to see the tiniest detail of good in

us; if he does not miss one sparrow falling to the ground (Mt 10:29), then he certainly will not be less attentive over us who are his blood-bought people. If the idea of God boasting over us seems pretty far fetched to you, then read Hebrews 11:16—'God is not ashamed to be called their God,' and Hebrews 2:11—'His is not ashamed to call them brethren.' We should be very careful that we do not unintentionally denigrate Calvary by refusing to accept God's sheer delight in us. If he went to such lengths to save us, he must regard us as extremely precious, warts and all!

Remember the old hymn by Frances Havergal: 'Take my life, and let it be consecrated, Lord, to Thee . . . Take my hands . . . my feet . . . my voice . . . my lips . . . my silver and my gold . . . my intellect . . . my will . . . my heart . . . my love. . . . Take myself, and I will be ever, only, all for Thee.' The Song of Solomon and this hymn-writer are both saying that if we give ourselves to Jesus, he will accept our offering, come into our heart, and take over our life, making it so good, fragrant and useful that all heaven will rejoice to see such people on the earth.

Chapter 7:10-13

These verses, speaking of the joyful anticipation and desire evidenced by the couple, could well describe the prelude to the consummation of the marriage of the Lamb (Rev 19:7-8). This should not just make us dream and wonder of course, rather it should cause us to rejoice and prepare ourselves for this glorious event.

I want to leave chapter 8 for you to explore, except to point out the loving appeal from the shepherd to his beloved in verse 6: 'Put me like a seal over your heart.' Jesus wants us to be so wholly his that he asks for proof of it from us. What is our response?

Pause and ponder

Such amazing and intimate love as described in the Song of Solomon requires a response. Why not respond now?

Part 2

Prayer

13

Bible Meditation and Prayer

These two disciplines belong together; they are both important to the development of our life with God. Meditation and quietness help us to understand the mind, will and feelings of God. Prayer leads us on from here to sense more accurately what he feels and what he wants us to do for and with him.

Prayer without Bible meditation can be mechanical, lacking the vitality which generally comes when we have freshly reviewed the Scriptures and thus entered into the feelings of the one who wrote them. For example, after meditating on Genesis 6:5-7, where God looked at the world and grieved over its rampant sin, we are more likely to feel the grief of God as he beholds the world today, with its appalling similarity, and therefore to pray more feelingly about the area of it in which we live. Again, after pondering Luke 15:7—'There will be more joy in heaven over one sinner who repents'—we are likely to pray more fervently that our friends might be saved so that all heaven may rejoice the more.

Prayer without Bible meditation can be a waste of time if we pour out our requests without pondering his word. Psalm 66:18 warns us: 'If I regard [cherish] wickedness in my heart, the Lord will not hear.' However, there is a remedy as David found: 'Thy word I have treasured in my heart, that I may not sin against Thee.' If we often meditate on the word, we are likely to pray effectively, because our hearts are pure enough for God to listen to us.

Prayer without Bible meditation can be unscriptural. If we do not pray in the name of Jesus (Jn 15:16), we will not receive any answers to our prayers. Constant meditation on Scripture, through which we see Jesus and discover God's truth, will cause us to know what the Lord can and cannot approve. Our Father will never agree to give us anything of which his Son disapproves.

The Holy Spirit is the inspirer and illuminator of the Scriptures, and when we study them together with him and ponder them in his company, he is more able to lead us into effective prayer. Paul says that we must 'pray at all times in the Spirit' (Eph 6:18), which means praying for that which conforms to God's will and desires. We can know the will of God, otherwise Paul would not have prayed for the Colossians 'that [they] may be filled with the knowledge of his will' (Col 1:9). The Holy Spirit 'searches all things, even the depths of God' (1 Cor 2:10), therefore he is the one to convey them to us, and thus inspire and instruct us in our praying. He usually does this by giving us a burden to pray, which is quite different from a fixation.

A fixation is something which we have seized upon because we want it done for our own welfare or satisfaction, but a burden is often unsought, perhaps even a surprise; it is an impelling (not compelling) of the Spirit, an urge to pray in a certain way, or for a certain person or situation. This urge stays with us, we cannot shed it, we pray with increasing feeling, even tears, though we cannot always give logical reasons as to why we do it.

When we are burdened, we pray on about the matter until God takes it away. How we need to spread our prayer lists before God and ask him to edit them. It could deliver us from a lot of prayers which God never initiated. The Holy Spirit loves to work together with us in this joyful discipline, and is always eager to help us, especially when we are weak. 'The Spirit also helps our weaknesses; for we do not know how to pray as we should, but the Spirit Himself intercedes for us' (Rom 8:26). He will do this for and with us if we continually immerse ourselves in the Bible and obey its laws, thus walking by the Spirit (Gal 5:16).

Meditation without prayer is incomplete. What is the point of pondering over the Bible without responding to its Author? God's great purpose in writing the Scriptures was to reveal himself to man as a God who desires fellowship and co-operation with him. He enjoys both of these when, after meditating, we pour out our hearts in fervent prayer.

George Mueller of Bristol found that he could not pray properly unless he first meditated on the Scriptures. He could not clearly discern the will of God without poring over the word, and he had no heart to pray unless the word had first kindled his spirit. When, after many years as a Christian, he discovered the vital link between these two disciplines, his whole ministry was transformed. The following extract from a biography of Mueller makes this clear:

> Particularly was this impression made on Mr. Mueller's mind and heart: that Whitfield's unparalleled success in evangelistic labours was plainly traceable to two causes and could not be separated from them as direct effects; namely, his unusual prayerfulness, and his habit of reading his Bible on his knees. . . . George Whitfield's life drove home the truth that God alone could create in him a holy earnestness to win souls and qualify him for such divine work by impart-

ing a compassion for the lost that should become an absorb-
ing passion for their salvation. And—let this be clearly
marked as another secret of this life of service—he now
began himself to read the Word of God upon his knees, and
often found for hours great blessing in such *meditation and
prayer* [my italics] over a single Psalm or chapter. . . . No
reader of God's Word can thus bow before God and His
open Book, without a feeling of new reverence for the
Scriptures, and dependence on their Author for insight into
their mysteries. . . . Again, such a habit naturally leads to
self-searching and comparison of the actual life with the
example and pattern shown in the Word. . . . The command challenges the conduct to appear for examination. . . . The words thus reverently read will be translated into the life, and mould the character into the image of
God. . . . The Holy Scriptures will suggest the very words
which become the dialect of prayer. . . . Here is the Spirit's
own inspired utterance, and, if the praying be moulded on
the model of His teaching, how can we go astray? . . . In
meditating over Hebrews 13:8, 'Jesus Christ the same yesterday today and forever,' translating it into prayer, he be-
sought God, with the confidence that the prayer was already
granted, that, as Jesus had already in His love and power
supplied all that was needful, in the same unchangeable love
and power He would so continue to provide. And so a
promise was not only turned into a prayer, but into a
prophecy—an assurance of blessing—a river of joy at once
poured into and flowed through his soul.[6]

We often talk about our 'quiet times', or periods of
prayer and Bible study. It is very important that they
actually do include time to be quiet before the Lord so
that he can speak to us, and time for the Holy Spirit to
enable us to digest the word so that it becomes part of
our daily life, as in George Mueller's case. Let's take a
closer look at those aspects of prayer, both private and
corporate, which link most obviously with Bible meditation. But before we do so, we'd better consider what

prayer is not.

Prayer is not the answer to everything, otherwise evangelism, church-planting, Bible study etc. would be superfluous. Prayer must accompany these activities; it must not be an escape from them. Prayer to heaven should result in power on earth, and this demands activity outside our buildings as well as prayer within them. A balance between the two will bring us into reality.

Prayer is not an activity possible only for spiritual heavyweights. A father does not only listen to his grown-up or most highly qualified children, likewise our Father listens to all of us in his family, however old or young we may be in the faith.

Prayer is not just spiritual first-aid in time of pain. If it is, then we have a most unreal relationship with God, and a very selfish one. Neither is it an attempt to placate a great deity up there in case he gets nasty. He does not need appeasing, and he never gets nasty; angry, yes, but vicious, never. There is no need whatsoever for us to go crawling into the presence of a dreadful God, grovelling before him in order to persuade him to give us a moment of his time and perhaps a little help. The moment we detect any reluctance to pray, or the feeling that we had better pray in order to keep on the right side of God, or that if we don't pray then disaster will strike us, we should cry out for help, step up our Bible meditation, and thus bring about a more balanced, and true, view of God.

Prayer involves two aspects which we should always hold in tension. There is a delightful intimacy which we are intended to enjoy with our heavenly Father, but equally there is respect and awe as we come into the presence of God. Although we can 'draw near with confidence to the throne of grace' (Heb 4:16) because of the one offering for sin for ever, we must never come lightly, for God is thrice holy, and even the seraphim must veil their eyes at the sight of him.

Prayer is both a privilege and a duty. Cherubim guard the throne, but there is no mention of their praying; seraphim attend the Most High constantly, but they do not seem to have the privilege of pleading the cause of man before him. Yet we are able to enjoy the privilege of fellowship with the very heart of this glorious God. We are given access, authority and opportunity; it is therefore a holy duty to take advantage of this, and an insult to neglect it. God has made us stewards of the world, heirs with his Son, confidantes of the Most High. It would be a crime to despise such an honour. Jesus said that we 'at all times ought to pray' (Lk 18:1), and Paul said, 'Pray without ceasing' (1 Thess 5:17). They both had a very high estimation of this priceless privilege, and they both practised what they preached. So, then, should we. How do you think God feels when he opens his throne room to us, the joint heirs with his Son, but finds that we cannot be bothered to come in?

Prayer is meant to be enjoyable, both to God and to us. God certainly enjoys and values real prayer. Revelation 8:3-5 seems to indicate that our prayers are stored up in heaven and that they open the way for God to accomplish his purposes on earth. They are described as incense, which indicates that our prayers are fragrant and enjoyable to God. If we really are in love with God, we should enjoy sharing with him, and a vital part of that sharing is prayer.

There are many aspects to prayer, so many that it is difficult to leave any of them out. As former leader of Intercessors for Britain, and until recently one of the leaders of Intercessors International, I am tempted to enlarge on spiritual warfare because of the great need of this nation. Never before has there been such a need for those who will rise up and seek God earnestly. Pagan

England needs mercy, and God will only grant it when his people show him that they mean business in their praying by engaging in it sacrificially. Why should God respond to the desultory, half-hearted prayers offered in the average prayer meeting? God looks for opportunities, given through our believing prayers, to send angels to the far corners of the world to crush disobedient evil spirits and to establish his rule. We were destined to work with God in this wonderful plan, so let's take a large dose of self-discipline and get on with it. However, much as I would like to enlarge on spiritual warfare, I have had to limit myself to those aspects of prayer which are particularly relevant to the subject of this book. I mention them briefly below, and will talk about them in greater depth in the following chapters.

The prayer meeting: Does God enjoy it? Do we?

Fellowship: This is characterized by intimate conversation and sharing between two people who love each other deeply.

Worship: Bible meditation should lead to adoration as we contemplate the one upon the throne and bow before him in wonder and praise.

Pleading: We are priests, pleading a case for others before the Judge.

Listening to God: We are members of an army receiving orders for battle, and servants waiting for orders from their Master. In order to hear those orders, we need to be quiet and listen.

Pause and ponder

A weak, dull prayer life is an insult to God and an obstacle to our spiritual growth. Bible meditation can revolutionize it, making it enjoyable for us and exciting and acceptable to God.

14

The Prayer Meeting

'Lord, do you enjoy the prayer meeting?' is a legitimate question for us to ask. Indeed, it is more important for us to ask this question than to wonder what we will get out of the meeting ourselves. Is there living worship? Are there times of quiet? What about honesty and reality, unity and faith? Do we have good leadership to keep us on course, and accurate information to keep our prayers specific? Do we witness signs and wonders from time to time? If these things are in evidence, then we can be sure that all heaven is enjoying the meeting.

Our personal Bible meditation can affect the corporate prayer meeting because of its transforming influence on our individual lives. We will be in a much better condition to share fellowship with the living God and with each other, and the increased sensitivity gained in our times of prayer alone will help us to pray together according to the mind of the Lord. It is important to set aside a time for meditation during the meeting. For example, the leader could read a passage such as Daniel 9, then everybody could read it together, picking out the most striking features of this glorious prayer. Then, after ten minutes of quiet reflection, folk could split into small groups to share their thoughts from the passage. The leader should call the people together again and lead them into prayer, or occasionally they should pray in the small groups. Keep the Bible open at the passage singled out for meditation, and remind one another from time to time of the main points so that direction is maintained. Reflecting like this on such a passage will surely raise up prayer for the nation. On another occasion a passage from chapter 5 of the Song of Solomon could be read, meditated on, and commented on, which would hope-fully inspire heartfelt worship leading to prayer. Again, chewing over Ephesians chapter 6 would help us to engage in true spiritual warfare.

In all this, so much depends on everyone coming prepared in heart, and on strong leadership by wise leaders. We need to come to the prayer meeting with our hearts full of the fruits of our meditations and with clean hands. We also need to have only one set of criteria for both our public and private prayer so that we are being honest and real, and sure of our direction, able to pray in unity and faith. Then we will be fighting fit, ready to worship, able to plead, likely to hear, and quick to delight our heavenly Father by our fellowship with him.

Prayer is carried on in the very presence of God, in the throne room, which is where we really belong. After the resurrection we shall live there for ever, but right now we have constant access to that place, for we have 'con-fidence to enter the holy place by the blood of Jesus' (Heb 10:19). Seeing that it was so costly to Jesus to make such access possible, it would be a crime to neglect such a privilege. Furthermore, there is a tremendous blessing to be gained there: 'How blessed is the one whom Thou dost choose, and bring near to Thee, to dwell in Thy courts. We will be satisfied with the goodness of Thy house, Thy holy temple' (Ps 65:4). It is helpful to regard the prayer meeting as a gathering around the throne of God, in his lovely house, and it is not wrong to use a little imagination, as long as it does not contradict Scripture, in order to envisage this.

Think of the angels crowding round, longing to look into the precious secrets which God is sharing with his dear people (1 Pet 1:12). They must be captivated by us as we stand in the beauty of holiness before God. Holiness is not tame and boring, but immensely exciting and beautiful. Father, Son and Holy Spirit are all with us; the whole Godhead is thrilled with us. If you doubt this, meditate on John 14:23. They pay keen attention to all that we share with them as long as it is genuine, and as long as we do not insult our great God with small prayers. God is interested to hear our opinions about, and our desires for, our neighbourhood and nation. He will want us to rejoice with him about the results of our contacts, outreaches and practical concern, and all the other things in which we are presumably working together with him.

In order to have a productive prayer meeting there needs to be a strong and sensitive leadership to cope with awkward people and to avoid bad habits. Leaders must be prepared to interrupt firmly and graciously, correct, insist on keeping direction, rebuke slanted prayer, 'deflate' the longwinded, and so on. They must encourage the timid, and curb the monopolists, who are usually proud individuals. Leaders must evaluate the use of spiritual gifts, exhorting those who are slack. They should also listen for the voice of God. All this may seem an impossible task for anyone, but there are godly and capable leaders who are able to tackle such a prospect. I have seen them at the Prayer and Bible Weeks which I led for some years, apart from many other conferences. When you find them, value them highly.

Some bad habits to avoid

It's very easy to fall into bad habits at prayer meetings. So that we can recognize and avoid them, I list some of the main offenders below.

Be real in your way of speaking. It is not natural to fall into seventeenth-century English and highly theological words. It may impress the speaker, but it usually scrambles the brains of newly saved people who end up feeling unable to compete. Again, some of our prayers display an apparent but quite unreal piety. We collect together all the most erudite phrases we know and trot them out either to the Lord or the congregation. Then again, there are the self-deprecating prayers of those who mumble, in a mournful voice, 'O Lord, I know I'm just a miserable sinner, worthless and weak . . .' as they wriggle through their depressing catalogue of iniquity. But do they realize that they are denying what Scripture says about the Christian?

The dreaded monologue is a one-way stream of words which defies interruption either by men or even by God. The stream is usually long, tedious and boring. Round the world in eighty minutes could describe the prayers of some zealous souls who feel that they had better give value for money while they have the floor. Whether the world benefits from such ministry will be best known when these prayers are played back in heaven, that is if they ever reached it.

Sometimes prayer is abused by using it as a back-handed way of letting other people know what you feel about them, while sheltering yourself under a kind of 'parliamentary immunity' as you appear to be talking to God. Two small boys gave an unwitting example of this after they had been fighting in the home. Their father took them to bed at night and, as was his custom, knelt down with an arm round both boys to pray with them.

He began by saying, 'Boys, God is not pleased with you when you fight, so I suggest you ask his forgiveness.' A long silence ensued, and much wriggling, but eventually one boy prayed, 'Lord Jesus, it is very, very, very wrong to fight; it is a terrible thing to fight; it's very wicked to fight; so I ask you to forgive my little brother for being so cruel and wicked to me.' We may laugh, but isn't it a little too close to the truth?

Do we use prayer to preach to God, telling him what he already knows? 'O Lord, as you know, Jesus died for us [as if he could ever forget].' Or, 'Lord, you said in Genesis 1:3, "Let there be light and there was light." Now, Lord, I want you to know that there is darkness in our street, the people there are sinful. O Lord, if only you knew what they are really like.' Believe it or not, I am actually quoting!

'Volume=power' is an equation not unknown in prayer meetings. Sadly, such people are often playing to the gallery in an attempt to impress others with their apparent godliness. Stentorian it may be, effective prayer it cannot be.

Why do so many of us adopt an artificial or affected manner of speaking as soon as the prayer meeting gets underway? It certainly doesn't impress God. A constant stream of 'Amens', 'Glorys' and 'Hallelujahs' in prayer meetings, together with those sort of mooing sounds, can be very distracting. Genuine and appropriate Amens etc. are good and right from time to time, but are they often a mere habit?

Shopping-list prayers are another bane. We can be very selfish in our prayer life—the 'give me' syndrome is not only found in the world. How must God feel as he looks out on a desperately needy world, longing to meet those needs, but hears only selfish prayers from those whom he chose to give out to others in sacrificial love?

Fear of man badly affects a prayer meering. Many

people say, 'I am too shy to pray in public,' or, 'If I pray, I might make a mess of it,' or, 'I can never find the right words.' My own experience may encourage you. I really wanted to pray in the prayer meeting, but I was hindered by all the fears mentioned above. However, on one famous occasion, I waited for a gap in the prayers with heart pounding. When I reckoned there was such a gap I shot to my feet to pray. What I did not know was that the girl behind me was sitting with her feet on the rung of my chair with her elbows on her knees and head in her hands. Consequently, when I shot up she collapsed in a heap on the floor, bringing others down with her. There was a most undignified heap of arms, legs, chairs etc., and I promptly fled. It was many weeks before I dared return, but with the help of a godly elder I was able to pray. I do not remember my prayer, but I spoke it out.

We need to acquire good habits, opposite to those above, in our prayer meetings, but these do not always come readily and immediately; we need to learn them as we gather together. It may be objected that we should never interrupt a person who is praying because that person is talking to God. Perhaps he is, but he is also affecting a whole group of other people. The long-winded will only learn to be short-winded if a leader reminds them that they have prayed for too long. The self-deprecating person will only learn to pray aright if he takes note of the leader who encourages him in public with scriptures which describe who he is in Christ. Those who indulge in back-handed prayers need to be roundly rebuked before everyone if they are not to continue in their sin of denigration. We can learn all these things together, as long as we have a humble and teachable spirit, and leaders who teach in love, grace and firmness. If some people walk out in a huff after correction, it proves that their attitude is not right. We should help them to detect their failing, and repent, and then welcome them back among us.

In our gatherings for prayer, then, let's make every effort to avoid bad habits, cultivate good ones, and so enjoy well-prepared, lively and exciting meetings in which God and man are delighted.

Pause and ponder

Through me, God can improve the prayer meeting.

15

Fellowship with God

In his first epistle John says that 'our fellowship is with the Father, and with His Son' (1 Jn 1:3). He speaks of the Son as one whom he has seen, touched and handled. Obviously, he had a close relationship with the one who was his Maker, but only because that one came near enough to make it possible. No stand-offish deity here, but a living, warm, vital God with a deep desire to commune with man—one of the main reasons why he created us.

I like the word 'sharing' as a definition of fellowship. Other words define it too, such as communion and friendship, but sharing emphasizes that fellowship, and prayer as part of fellowship is a two-way thing: a dialogue rather than a monologue; the outpouring of one heart to another; the attentive listening by one to the other. Mutual enjoyment of each other's company, and the sharing of plans, griefs and joys common to both are all part of this wonderful relationship. Jesus, the head of the church, appeals for such fellowship with us. He does not beg for it—he does not need to seeing that he is Lord of all—but with great courtesy and grace he *asks* to come into our hearts. It is thrilling to realize that we can give God something which he enjoys and appreciates, and it must surely make our heart leap as we give him what he asks for.

Fellowship is relationship

Many people say the Lord's Prayer on Sunday, addressing God as 'our Father.' But how can he be our Father if we have never been accepted as his children? Some years ago when I was a pastor, my wife was speaking at a women's meeting while I was supposed to be looking after our children at home. I got immersed in a book and left the children to play upstairs, but suddenly the noise up there reached a crescendo and I felt I ought to investigate. When I got upstairs I discovered thirteen children there and the room looking as though a typhoon had hit it. I selected our own three children and threw out the rest. They had no right to be in my house because they were not my flesh and blood. I had no obligation to provide for them, help them or even speak to them, for they were not my family at all. Similarly, God knows every single child of his, but he has no obligation to respond to those who have never 'received Him' and therefore been given 'the right to become children of God' (Jn 1:11–14).

God only opens heaven, his home, to those who have the right to be there and who are able to live there because they have eternal life. Such people have a right relationship with God, one in which they reverence him and respect him while at the same time enjoy him as their Father. Many figures of speech are employed to describe our relationship with God—a bride, an army, priests, a temple, servants, friends—but the primary one is probably that of children because the term highlights the fact that we have our Father's life, the 'divine seed'

(1 Pet 1:23; 2 Pet 1:4). Without that we could not enter any
of the other descriptions for the church—in fact, we could not be born again at all.

Fellowship is a privilege to be guarded

The precious privilege of fellowship needs to be jealously guarded. The presence of God is a holy place, purity is its atmosphere, and although we are welcome there because we are his priests, we still need to lift up hands which are holy and clean. God insists on clean hands. 'Who may ascend into the hill of the Lord?' asks the Psalmist, continuing, 'He who has clean hands and a pure heart' (Ps 24:3–4).

Some children were playing in the garden after a heavy rainstorm, revelling in the glutinous mud, quite oblivious of the state of hands, face and feet. But on their attempt to get back into the home, they were very firmly prevented until hands, face and feet were clean enough to satisfy the parents. A homely story, but one offering a spiritual lesson. Do you greet a holy God with mucky hands? A clean God loves clean children, but, having said that, no one will ever be totally spotless here on earth as God well knows. King David was not perfect, yet God called him a man after his own heart. The reason for this is found in the attitude of David's heart: he was keenly aware of his weakness, but continually reached out to God in sincere love, earnestly seeking to keep his hands as clean as possible. God is demanding, but he is not unmerciful or unrealistic He will never lower his standards, but he will always be an understanding and forgiving Father to the children he knows so well.

Fellowship is surrender

Complete surrender is a fundamental part of our relationship with God. Romans 12:1–2 is a powerful plea for our will to be in line with our Father's will. Jesus surrendered his will to his Father and thus set an example for us to follow. He will never surrender his will to us, for he is the supreme, all-knowing and holy God; every time it is our will which must bend to his. God has nothing to say to rebels except repent, and he does not listen to the prayers of those who play with sin: 'If I regard wickedness in my heart, the Lord will not hear' (Ps 66:18).

Our will is usually the last thing to be surrendered to God, and it often happens in stages. The desire to have our own way and to run our own lives is terribly strong; it causes us to waste a lot of time as we grudgingly hand ourselves over to the control of the Lord, piece by piece. How many people drop into hell, I wonder, during the time we waste struggling against the will of God? Satan tries to deceive us into imagining God as a demanding selfish God, determined to rob us of most of life's pleasures and to crush us into submission, and like fools we fall for it, instead of seeing the very different picture which Scripture paints. There we see a God vitally interested in the fulfilment of our destiny; one who with infinite love and care has charted our course, and who reaches out to lead us into our highest good. His only stipulation is that we should hold his hand, in other words, join our will to his.

Fellowship is broken by disobedience

Disobedience mars our relationship with God. The Apostle John said, 'The one who says, "I have come to know Him [share fellowship with him]," and does not keep His commandments, is a liar' (1 Jn 2:4). Walking with God is walking with the truth. Disobedience is characteristic of the devil, the father of lies, and when we persist on this course we walk with Satan. Let me put it this way. If we are happily walking arm in arm with God, then we are walking in the paths of righteousness, because he never walks anywhere else. But if we then get distracted by some temptation and decide to respond to it, we disengage our arm from his and tell him to go on ahead while we catch up later, and we then proceed in totally the opposite direction from the way in which God is walking.

If this wandering around and backtracking illustrates your present conduct, I urge you seriously to consider who it is you are actually walking with. Remember that God is so merciful that he will abundantly pardon those who have been guilty of treachery, as long as they turn round and walk again with him. Jesus said, 'If you love Me, you will keep My commandments' (Jn 14:15). In these words he gives us a prime reason for obedience: our love for him. Our obedience is the greatest testimony the world can know of the reality of our fellowship with God. How beautifully Mary summed up the pathway to fellowship with him when she simply said, 'Whatever He says to you, do it' (Jn 2:5).

Fellowship is broken by disunity

I have already pointed out that disobedience breaks our fellowship with God, but so does strife between fellow Christians. John is quite clear about this: 'The one who says he is in the light and yet hates his brother is in the darkness until now' (1 Jn 2:9). Walking with God means walking in the light; strife with a brother or sister means walking in the darkness. Fellowship with God and disunity with our brethren are totally incompatible.

The prophet Amos said, 'Do two men walk together unless they have made an appointment [a heart agreement]?' (Amos 3:3). I must sadly confess that I have disagreed with God more than once, and I have also done the same with my brethren. In both cases, fellowship stops and there is no working together unless, and until, there is reconciliation. When that takes place it is like pouring out precious oil before the Lord, as described in Psalm 133. Such reconciliation is fragrant to God, and causes him to bless us.

I once had a dream where huge groups of people were gathered around the Lord. He was looking at each group with mingled love and grief. I then saw the reason for his attitude: each group was trying to push the others aside saying, 'You cannot use them, Lord, for they have sinned against us. We are walking in the truth, but they have a spirit of error. Judge them, Lord, for their refusal to agree with us.' Focusing in, I saw two brothers standing before the Lord. One would viciously push the other aside while maintaining an expression of devotion upon his face as he turned towards the Lord; then the other would do precisely the same thing. Each one said, 'O Lord, you know that I am walking with you; receive my worship, O loving Father. But do not be fooled by the hypocrisy of my poor deceived brother who has gone astray.' How sad that each one thought he was walking in the light when in fact both were walking in darkness. How could God possibly bless them and use them? And how could he share fellowship with them?

Fellowship is broken by the spirit of the world

The Amplified Bible definition of worldliness is particularly good: 'craving for sensual gratification, greedy longings of the mind, assurance in one's own resources or stability of earthly things' (see 1 Jn 2:16). We were born again to live in a radically different way. We are to be like salt in this corrupt world, and we are to dispel its darkness with our light. We are called to battle against the Enemy, exposing all his schemes to destroy the fabric of society. However, we are in constant danger of succumbing to the relentless pressure to conform to this world, and it would be a brave Christian indeed who says he is never tempted to join the rat race. Our safety lies in our fellowship with God, especially in our prayer life and Bible meditation.

Love of the world hinders our relationship with the Father, and can therefore nullify our prayer life (1 Jn 2:15). In the days when I was a young Christian we were told that worldliness was smoking, drinking, wearing make-up (I never did), and going to pubs. If you were truly holy you were even suspicious of wine gums! Although there may be some truth in the above observation, it is rather a simplistic and legalistic approach, and one that falls into the trap of concentrating on externals. Worldliness is found in the heart before it ever becomes visible in the conduct. Jesus said that murder, adultery, slander etc. come from the heart (Mt 15:19). Selfishness, greed and pride are all found in the church as well as the world. With these heart attitudes, no wonder the church is so weak and ineffective in her conduct. She needs the power of God, but this power is not a divine commodity doled out to those who clamour for a supply, but that which is imparted from God to his people when they are close enough for him to do so. Close fellowship with God gives access to real power, while fellowship with the world leads to weakness. Christ's church is only strong when her members are in close and vital touch with the head, filled with love for him and 'hating even the garment polluted by the flesh' (Jude 23), i.e. completely opposed to any form of worldliness, however small.

Enjoyed or endured?

Some of the priests described in the book of Malachi regarded their God-given privilege as a wearisome task. They had the joy of bringing offerings from the people to God which would cover their sins until Jesus took them away for ever at Calvary. They stood between the living and the dead; their ministry helped to preserve the lives of the Israelites; they were closer to God than anyone else at that time; yet they endured rather than enjoyed their privilege. David, in contrast, could not get enough of God. Fellowship with God was the joy of his heart, the stuff of life, his reason for living. Psalm 63 records the great longing of his soul for the living God. Perhaps you feel more like the priests than David, but take heart, you can change. However, you must first want to change. How important is fellowship with God to you? He is, after all, the Maker of heaven and earth, the Shepherd and Guardian of your soul, the one who offered himself without spot to God because he could not bear to see you going to hell. Once you have decided you really do want this fellowship above everything else, how do you go about it?

First, as in Bible meditation, make time—you will never find it. Look for minutes rather than hours initially —this is more realistic. Ephesians 5:16 advises us to make the most of our time. He is a fool who thinks that this will be a cheap transaction or an easy process. Jesus said, 'Seek first [not nearly first] his kingdom' (Mt 6:33). Here we are face to face with the gritty aspect of our glorious Christian life; it is not a life for the comfort-seeker, nor does God ever offer us a quick route to maturity. He looks for those who will be ruthless with their fleshly desires, and cold-bloodedly disciplined in their stewardship of the time which is only given to them once. We shall only tread this pathway once; we have only one life to live, one chance to fulfil our destiny. Time is God's training-ground for eternity; to use it well is to invest in eternity; and what better way to use it than in fellowship with God. To misuse time is to lose the opportunity of laying up treasure in heaven (eternity). Life time is entrusted to man; prime time is for the King!

Secondly, as in Bible meditation, find a place. There is no need to be superstitious about this, as if the place becomes a shrine, but many people find that a particular room or chair, or maybe a summer-house or a park is conducive to prayer time. Mrs Wesley is reputed to have put her apron over her head when praying, and that became her 'place'. A friend of mine finds a race-course is his trysting-place with God (though not during the actual races!). A former landlord of mine used to pray in the airing cupboard in the bathroom because it was warm and quiet (I discovered this during my bath one evening!). My own favourite place for prayer while at Bible college was on a small hill nearby, where I used to kneel in the early hours of the morning. It had one tree on it which reminded me of Calvary, and from that vantage point I could see the whole town. It was not always solemn. One cold misty morning I wrapped myself in a grey blanket and prayed in a loud voice walking up and down, quite oblivious of the chicken farmer who was feeding the hens rather early. I have never seen a man so terrified; he ran off with a scream, and my prayer was somewhat abbreviated! But I did pray for him.

Some people can pray in the midst of a commotion and do not need a particular place; others cannot bear a disturbance. Whatever our temperament, it is essential to make time for God and to find a conducive place if we need one. Our flesh will moan and groan, and we are likely to find all kinds of excuses as to why we cannot maintain our prayer life, but our excuses will sound very hollow at the judgement seat of Christ. As an incentive to fellowship with God, read the Song of Solomon 2:14. Listen to the heart's desire of your Bridegroom, and if you love him, respond. Why not do so now?

Thirdly, learn to be still (Ps 46:10). The NASB margin reads: 'Relax, let go,' but what a job it can be to do so! But this is precisely where Bible meditation can help our prayer life. If we are persevering in it, it will be teaching us to be more patient, still and thorough, allowing more time for God to speak to us through his word. This will help us to be more careful and studied in our approach to our prayer life; our prayers will be more thoughtful and more accurate. Everything in the modern world militates against being still. Wherever we go there is noise and rush—music blares from transistor radios and cars. However, it can be done. Help is needed, but it is offered by no less than the Holy Spirit of God. Being still does not mean making the mind inactive, it means turning our thoughts to the one from whom comes peace, and reining in the mind when it wanders just as we would rein in a horse. As we do our part in this way, the Spirit will do his by giving revelation. He knows that our minds, conditioned by our western culture, need help, but he is ever willing to teach us the art of meditating on the Lord as we search the Scriptures, looking for him.

Fellowship is based on honesty

Real fellowship is based on honesty. It is heart-to-heart stuff, and hypocrisy spoils it. A pastor was standing by the church door greeting his flock. He asked each in turn, 'How are you?' and they all, without exception, replied, 'Fine thanks.' After weeks of this he decided that by the law of averages alone it could not be true that they were all fine all the time, so he called the church together for a straight talk. He said, 'Friends, you are a bunch of evangelical liars. Every week you tell me that

you're fine, when you know that is not true. In future tell
me how you really are, please.' He was somewhat be-
mused the following Sunday when they all left by the
rear door. When they eventually started to use the front
door again, he asked one man how he was and he said,
'Fine . . . er . . . oh dear!' and then burst into tears,
confessing that he had quarrelled with his wife before the
meeting and was in an awful state. How lovely it was to
pray for him and see him rush home to be reconciled.

But can I be honest with God? Dare I tell him the
whole truth? Dare I grumble? This depends on our concept of God. While I must always remember that he is
holy and the Creator, I should not forget that he is my
Father. In these days of broken families, it may be difficult for some to know what a true father is really like,
and in some cases even who their father is at all, but an
examination of scriptures such as Psalm 103:13, and
Matthew 7:9–11 can be a great help.

A true father is unshockable, he will always listen to
his children, even when they 'blow their top'. It may
anger him, but he will not crush them with a rebuke, nor
will he cease to love them. He will listen quietly and then
pinpoint the reasons for their outburst. He will not be
shocked at their attitude, because he is too experienced
in the ways of man. His whole desire will be to help his
children get out of their hearts all that wounds or em-
bitters them, everything which spoils them or distorts
their perception of things.

God is like that. When David said, in Psalm 142:2, 'I
pour out my complaint before Him,' God did not
rebuke him, nor shut him up, nor strike him dead. God
can stand the test of our grumbling—he has had
centuries of experience, after all. Some people say, 'I
feel so angry inside, but I dare not say so to God.' How
foolish to think that we can hide anything from him any-
way (see Ps 139:7–12). Where is the place where God is

not? Who can hide anything at all from the one who made everything? If he numbers the hairs of our heads, he will certainly keep track of all our thoughts. Jesus knew the thoughts of his disciples even when he was man, so what hope is there of hiding them from the risen Christ?

It is far wiser to be honest with God and express our anger and frustration. He is totally unshockable, infinitely merciful, well able to cope with even our vilest thoughts. Expressing such thoughts will not bring down a divine thunderbolt. When we bring them into the light of God they will die in the same way in which microbes from a dark cave die the moment they are exposed to light. God can stand it, even if our loved ones can't. After practising the above, I always feel a sense of healthy shame and have a better perspective of things, which enables me to get on with God's great work with a stronger heart.

Having said this, it is as well for us to remember Numbers 14:27: God overheard the continual grumbling and complaining of the Israelites, and it angered him. The habit of murmuring can be dangerous. Pouring out the heart as part of keeping short accounts with God is one thing, continuous complaining is another.

Pause and ponder

I can give God something he really wants—my fellowship. Surely I should not rob him?

16

Worship

God loves true worship, indeed he greatly desires it.
Jesus said that 'true worshipers shall worship the
Father in spirit and truth; for such people the Father
seeks to be His worshipers' (Jn 4:23–24). He empha-
sized this when he taught his disciples to pray: 'Hallowed
[exalted above all; distinguished from all else; eulogized]
be Thy name' (Mt 6:9).

Worship is a very great occupation, not only down
here, but in heaven too. The angels and other inhabitants of heaven seem to spend most of their time bowing
down to magnify God (cf. Rev 5:8–14). They must therefore spend much time meditating on him. In the light of
this, I must point out that a mere spiritual singsong is no
substitute for real worship, and God instantly senses the
difference between them. Malachi rebuked the priests
for bringing shoddy offerings to the Lord's house, and
asked them if they really thought that God would accept
them. He also warned them not to rob God (Mal 1:6–14;
3:8). Shouldn't we, then, be equally careful to come to
our meetings with hearts truly prepared and worship
which is genuine and of a high quality?

My ministry has involved visiting hundreds of churches and fellowships, all of which have a 'time of worship' during their services; some are very good times, but others are very poor. There may be excellent musicianship, energetic leaders, lovely tunes, but no sense of the Spirit. It is sometimes a performance before the people rather than an offering to God. The main reason for thin worship is, I believe, a lack of preparation of heart. Scripture exhorts us to get ready for our meetings with God. 1 Corinthians 14:26 says: 'When you assemble, each one has a psalm, has a teaching, has a revelation, has a tongue, has an interpretation. Let all things be done for edification.' If we have all been meditating, praying, and paying attention to our spiritual condition, then we shall come together with a glorious succession of offerings to God which will please and honour him. In some traditions no opportunity is given for such a free-flowing time, but where there is, let us take advantage of it.

Some good books are available on the subject of worship, therefore I will only touch on it in this chapter. Graham Kendrick's excellent book *Worship* (Kingsway Publications, 1984) has helped many of us improve our worship.

Several Greek words illustrate different aspects of worship. One is *proskuneo*, meaning 'to reverently draw near to kiss'. Those who meditate on the glory of God's character will often find themselves doing this. They will emulate those who 'fell down and worshipped God who sits on the throne saying, "Amen. Hallelujah!"' (Rev 19:4), and the three wise men who 'fell down and worshiped him; and presented to Him gifts of gold and frankincense and myrrh' (Mt 2:11). No shoddy offerings there!

In one of the churches where I served as pastor, we were singing a song: 'O come let us worship and bow down.' As we sang, the Spirit of God caused us literally to bow down. Some of us wept, including myself as I saw the bread and wine on the table, for it reminded me of the sheer majesty of the one who shattered the power of the enemy at the cross. The presence of God was so powerful that I and some others ended up on our faces before him. There was such a sense of awe that we spent the rest of the time in silence. Eventually it was broken by the sobs of some who had realized how ingrained sin was in their lives, and who were now desperately anxious to be clean. My reason for telling this story is that before this meeting we had spent more time than usual in heart preparation, prayer and fasting. It paid off. It produced real worship. In Acts 13:2 the leaders of the church in Antioch were 'ministering to the Lord and fasting'; there was a sacrificial element to their ministry to the Lord, it was not cheap. Presumably part of their ministry was in prayer too.

Another Greek word for worship is *methusko*, which means 'intoxicated' or 'transported'. At Pentecost the disciples were worshipping with such extravagant joy and abandon that they were accused of being drunk (Acts 2:3–4, 13). Indeed they were—in the Spirit—but they were not disorderly. God and man were enjoying each other. God rejoices with all his heart over his people (Zeph 3:17). King David 'was dancing before the Lord with all his might' (2 Sam 6:14) as part of his worship on one occasion. His outbursts of worship in Psalms 145–150 contain the most extravagant praise. There is nothing to be ashamed of in worshipping in an un-British fashion, as long as it is genuine. There is nothing wrong in exuberance—it is an integral part of worship—but we should remember that other aspects of worship involve bowing down, repentance, renewed obedience, accepting judgement or chastening. We must keep all these different aspects in fine balance.

The other Greek work is *latrueo*, meaning 'work' or 'serve'. It is a reminder that we can truly worship God by doing a job well. Paul urged the church at Corinth: 'Whether, then, you eat or drink or whatever you do, do all to the glory of God' (1 Cor 10:31). In other words, let your service be an act of worship.

In the great art of worship, Bible meditation and prayer go hand in hand; in fact, one depends on the other. Without meditation, worship is shallow, for it does not come from a heart freshly envisioned and stirred through the word. Many people in Bible times worshipped God after contemplating his glory, David pre-eminently so—a look through the Psalms will give ample proof of that. It seems to me that it was after much contemplation and prayer that Job worshipped God with those sublime words: 'Though He slay me, I will hope in Him' (Job 13:15). And, after more prayer and thought, he cried out in costly worship again in Job 19:25; 'I know that my Redeemer lives.' It seems likely to me that it was during a time of prayer and contemplation that Abraham worshipped God by his willingness to offer up his only son Isaac as an offering to him. If we were to spend more time pondering Calvary, praying on the basis of what we glean from that sublime account, our worship would have a greater depth and reality. It is for this that I would plead.

Pause and ponder

If my offerings of worship are shoddy, why should God accept them? But they can improve, if I think of him more often and in greater depth.

17

Pleading with God

Pleading does not mean trying to wheedle something out of a reluctant God, as if he was a grudging Father. If he 'did not spare His own Son . . . will He not also with Him freely give us all things?' (Rom. 8:32) He can hardly be called ungenerous. Nevertheless, he is also the God who will be enquired of, and the one who says, 'Come now, and let us reason together' (Is 1:18) and, 'Let us argue our case together, state your cause, that you may be proved right' (Is 43:26), and again, 'Plead your case before the mountains . . . because the Lord has a case against His people . . . What have I done to you? . . . Answer Me' (Mic 6:1–3).

God is generous, but he is also rational. He expects intelligent and heartfelt arguments from us his priestly intercessors. Some prayers are intelligent but not heart-felt, the reason often being a lack of real meditation on the people and cases for which we are pleading in prayer. How many of us spend time contemplating the awful condition of the lost? How many then approach the throne with loud crying and tears, as Jesus did, to find grace for those we pray for? A measure of identification with the person or situation in view is necessary for those who plead a case. This was shown by Moses. Pleading for the people of Israel he said, 'But now, if Thou wilt, forgive their sin—and if not, please blot me out from Thy book' (Ex 32:32). He cared so deeply that he would have perished with them if necessary. Note, too, that he argued the case with God, and God did the same. The life of an unsaved person is largely wasted when we see it in the context of eternity, and a wasted life is the ultimate tragedy. If we ponder more deeply the prayers in the Bible, the needs of our neighbours, the tragedy of a lost destiny, and the feelings of Jesus, then we will feel more deeply and thus pray more powerfully.

Those who spend time in prayer and Bible meditation will become increasingly aware of the presence of God, and will realize that heaven is not only God's home, but a courtroom as well (see Job 1:6–12). There are trials going on in heaven. To take part in this holy activity we must be fit to plead, we must understand court procedure, and we must have our brief prepared. Our meditations will make us aware not only of God's holy hatred of evil, but also his deep feelings towards those 'in the dock' who have been ensnared by it. In turn, we are expected to enter into God's feelings and pour out our hearts to him (Ps 62:8). As we do so we will find ourselves sharing our hearts with others too. Scripture indicates that intelligent argument should be combined with deep feeling: 'I urge that entreaties and prayers . . . be made' (1 Tim 2:1). This is pleading with God. We may not have the feelings straightaway, in fact sometimes we need to start in cold blood, but the crucial thing is to start.

In a court there is a judge. Abraham refers to God as 'the Judge of all the earth' (Gen 18:25), and Peter describes Jesus as the 'Judge of the living and the dead' (Acts 10:42). There is also someone on trial whose actions and words are carefully weighed. We are being watched and weighed all the time. Proverbs 15:3 tells us that 'the eyes of the Lord are in every place, watching the evil and the good', and Romans 14:12 declares that 'each one of us shall give account of himself to God.'

An accuser is present in court. Satan is our accuser (Rev 12:10), constantly seeking to denigrate us before our Father. He will always condemn and accuse, seeking to destroy. Of course, God may accuse us too, but there is a great difference. God accuses us to convict and deliver, never to destroy. Every accused person needs an advocate, meaning one who is able to plead a case on our behalf. Jesus is described as our advocate in 1 John 2:1, the word translated 'advocate' meaning 'one called alongside to help' in the original Greek. Romans 8:33–34 puts it beautifully: 'Who will bring a charge against God's elect? God is the one who justifies; who is the one who condemns? Christ Jesus . . . who intercedes for us.' Who needs to be afraid with such a counsel for the defence? However, only Christians have this counsel. What about our friends who do not know Christ? Jesus asks us to co-operate with him in the work of bringing them to saving faith in himself, their advocate.

A verdict is given at a trial. To the lost the following verdict is given: 'Let the one who does wrong, still do wrong; and let the one who is filthy, still be filthy' (Rev 22: 11). God does not say this vengefully; he simply confirms the decision which the unsaved have made, whether they made it very deliberately or by neglect and indifference. After the verdict has been declared, either a punishment is handed out or a celebration ensues, depending on the assessment made by a wholly just God as to whether those in the dock took advantage of eternal safety or not.

Now let's apply the above sketch to the matter of meditation and pleading in our Christian experience day by day. Christians are 'a royal priesthood' (1 Pet 2:9); Christ 'has made us to be . . . priests to His God and

Father' (Rev 1:6). Part of the early priests' work was 'to offer both gifts and sacrifices' (Heb 8:3) for the people. Now, of course, there are no actual sacrifices to offer because Jesus offered that 'one sacrifice for sins for all time' (Heb 10:12). But the priests also made intercession for the people, which means that they stood before God on behalf of others in order to plead their case. Moses' action on behalf of the people of Israel is an example of this (Ex 32:30–35).

We are called to go into the presence of God to do the same for our generation. Priests are advocates (those called alongside to help), and advocates are expected to learn the condition and circumstances of their clients so that they can present powerful pleas on their behalf in the court of the judge. Some of the people recorded in Scripture can instruct us in this holy art, for example: Abraham (Gen 18:16–33), Moses (Ex 32:30–35; 33: 12–16), Solomon (2 Chron 6: 14–42), Job (Job 13:3, 15; 23:3–7), God himself (Is 43:26), and Amos (Amos 7:1–9).

As we persevere in the art of pleading a case before God, we will often find that a sense of burden develops: we cannot let go of a matter, our heart weeps and our spirit cries. But God sometimes removes this burden, and we must not allow conscience to make us try to retain it. We should, therefore, pray on while a sense of burden remains, and stop when it ceases. When pleading for a loved one who is unsaved, it is very important to remember that in the last analysis a person's will is the deciding factor. If God refuses to cut across the human will, then neither can we.

One of the great intercessors of the last century was George Mueller. He has much to teach us in this matter of pleading, as the following extract shows:

Mark his [Mueller's] manner of pleading. He used argument

in prayer, and at this time he piles up eleven reasons why God should and would send help. This method of holy argument, ordering our cause before God as an advocate would plead before a judge, is not only a lost art, but to many it actually seems puerile. And yet it is abundantly taught and exemplified in Scripture. Abraham in his plea for Sodom is the first great example of it. Moses excelled in this art, in many crises interceding on behalf of the people, with consummate skill, marshalling arguments as a general marshals battalions. Elijah on Carmel is a striking example of power in this special pleading . . . Of course God does not need to be convinced: no argument can make any plainer to Him the claims of trusting souls to His intervention, claims based upon His own words, confirmed by His oath. And yet He will be enquired of and argued with. That is His way of blessing. He loves to have us set before Him our cause and His own promises; He delights in the well ordered plea, where argument is piled on argument. See how the Lord Jesus commended the persistent argument of the woman of Canaan, who, with the wit of importunity actually turned His own objection into a reason . . . catching the Master Himself in His words, as He intended she should, and turning His apparent reason for not granting into a reason for granting her request . . . He said, 'Be it unto you as you will.'

So Mueller concludes: 'We are to argue our case with God, not to convince Him, but ourselves. In proving to Him that, by His own oath, word and character, He has bound Himself to interpose, we demonstrate to our own faith that He has given us the right to ask and claim, and that He will answer our plea because He cannot deny Himself.'[7]

This dear man must now be known in heaven as one who pleaded effectively with God on behalf of others. May we also be known there for the same reason.

Pause and ponder

Heaven waits to hear my pleading. As I do so, angels

learn, demons tremble, people are delivered, and God is delighted.

18

Listening to God

Listening is an important part of our fellowship with God, both in prayer and Bible meditation. Reading the Bible, studying it, and memorizing it are all essential in meditation, but unless we are listening to God through it all, there is not much point in the exercise. Similarly, we may make time for prayer, find a quiet place, and plead our case, but unless we listen we will miss God's voice and conclude that he hasn't heard us and cannot answer us, and we will go away disappointed. Listening, then, is essential for fellowship, and it is dangerous to ignore it. Proverbs 1:33 says: 'But he who listens to me shall live securely, and shall be at ease from the dread of evil.' Putting this into practice proves that we are true children and real servants of God, and that we know where our safety lies.

The injunction 'Stop, look, listen!' often given to our small children at the kerb, could well be given to us as God's children by the Holy Spirit. In fact, he does use all these words in Scriptures when describing prayer.

Stop

In Psalm 46:10 God actually commands us: 'Be still' (NIV). Being still involves stopping what we are doing in order to concentrate on something more important. The burning bush was used by God to make Moses stop so that he could hear God instructing him about his future. If Moses had not stopped, he would not have heard, and thousands of Israelites would have had no leader. Think what could happen if you do not stop and listen. Paul's experience on the Damascus road served the same divine purpose. Paul was an extraordinary man, so God used extraordinary means to make him stop and listen. If Paul had not stopped and heard God, it is possible that we would never have heard the gospel. God, in his ruthless love, brings his children in every age to a halt from time to time so that he can gain their attention, speak clearly to them, and help to keep their feet on straight paths.

Look

We should always be 'looking unto Jesus' (Heb 12:2, Authorized Version), 'fixing our eyes on Jesus' as the New American Standard Bible puts it. This verse, and others such as Isaiah 42:1—'Behold, My Servant,' are divine injunctions which demand a response. Looking is a doing word, a conscious act of our will. If our eyes are on the Son of God through Bible meditation, our concept of God will deepen and we will be more likely to turn consciously to a real Person when we pray, and therefore we will be more real in our praying and more able to listen to him. We will also understand more clearly what God wants us to know. Such 'looking' makes us God-conscious and sensitive to his will.

Listen

Listening to God, as I have already said, is a vital aspect of both prayer and Bible meditation. Both disciplines were seen in the life of Jesus, who also listened intently to his Father. All who truly follow him, therefore, must listen to God.

Consider the habit of his life mentioned prophetically in Isaiah 50:4—'Morning by morning, He awakens My ear to listen.' I believe that Jesus spent as much time listening to his Father as he did speaking to him. No wonder God said of him, 'This is my beloved Son, in whom I am well-pleased' (Mt 3:17). He had no trouble directing his Son. Jesus said, 'The son can do nothing of Himself, unless it is something He sees the Father doing' (Jn 5:19), and, 'As I hear, I judge' (Jn 5:30). Such rapt attention enabled God to do whatever he wanted through his obedient, attentive Son. What divine economy! But don't let's simply admire Jesus for doing it, let's do it too!

It is costly to listen to God. It is significant that Samuel was offering a sacrifice when he 'cried to the Lord for Israel and the Lord answered him' (1 Sam 7:9). Our sacrifice may be the TV, hobbies, a night out, or even Christian fellowship if it prevents us from getting to our quiet place to hear God. This will not be easy in our fast-moving world where we are used to instant service and constant noise. Such a world does not lend itself to quietness. Many people today are actually afraid of quietness. A teenager once said to me, 'I dare not be quiet, I would have to think, and in the nuclear age that is too frightening.' The spirit of the world creeps into the church and makes it nervous of silence. I do not mean an awkward silence, but the silence which makes a way for the Lord to speak to his people, and which heightens our expectation of hearing him as we give him a chance to speak.

We are not used to being quiet, either in our private prayer times or public meetings. Even when our leaders say, 'Let us have a moment's quiet,' it usually is only a moment. A friend's small son used his new stopwatch to time such a moment and discovered that the average was 10.2 seconds; the longest prayer, by the way, was 13.4 minutes! His behaviour should not be encouraged, of course, but his observations could teach us a thing or two. I wrote in chapter 14 about the prayer meeting, but it would be good to note one or two things here about silence.

First, leaders of prayer meetings must lose their fear of silence, resisting the temptation to fill it with a chorus or a 'gap-fill' prayer, which usually means nothing to God or man. It needs courage to make room for, and to maintain, silence in order to wait on God, but it is always worth it. If leaders are embarrassed about silence, and urging a constant stream of prayer, they will train the people to be the same, and then the Holy Spirit will not be able to speak and work in the way he wants to.

Secondly, before entering a time of silence, we need a focus. It is no use waiting on the Sovereign of all sovereigns with an empty or unfocused mind, and what better scripture to choose than one which speaks clearly about Jesus as a real person. Jeremiah 23:18 speaks of standing (waiting) 'in the council of the Lord'; obviously, then, we should be looking at and listening to that Lord as we wait for him to speak to us. If you have an audience with the Queen (I do not speak from experience), you do not initiate the conversation but listen attentively first until she invites you to answer. During this time your gaze will not be wandering all over the place, but fixed intently on the Queen. Listening is a sign of our respect.

Waiting on God

It seems that one meaning of the phrase 'waiting on God' is 'being entwined with God' or 'clinging to God.' This is a lovely concept. It reminds me of the scripture which says, 'The gate is small, and the way is narrow that leads to life' (Mt 7:14). Once we have passed through that gate, and placed our hand in God's, we embark on a dangerous and demanding journey. When Jesus says, 'Follow me,' he does not mean that we just fall in behind him and trail along. He stretches out his hand saying, 'Walk side by side with me; hold on because your safety depends on it; only I know the way, for I have trodden it before.' So, when God tells us, 'Blessed is the man . . . watching daily at my gates' (Prov 8:34), he is not suggesting that we just hang around. This waiting is an alert, attentive attitude in which we are expecting our Master to tell us things. Such waiting on God is a sign of our servanthood; indeed, the phrase is meant to remind us of the servant aspect of our relationship with God.

Psalm 123:2 describes the right attitude of a servant to his master: 'As the eyes of servants look to the hand of their master . . . so our eyes look to the Lord our God.' Although this verse speaks of eyes, it infers that the servants will listen as well as look, for they pay close attention to the look and the command of their master. God is never in a hurry, for he inhabits eternity. Often we are too time bound, losing a true perspective of life. God also loves our fellowship, and he wants us to linger in his presence too. We are his sons and daughters, but we are also his servants; we are free and welcome to come into his presence, but bound also to wait on him. God does not want us to remain as spiritual infants, but to mature into responsible and obedient servants. Therefore he causes us not only to wait *on* him till he instructs us, but often *for* him as the months or years go by before he actually does what he promised us. Time's years are eternity's seconds.

God is waiting to speak to us, but he may find it hard to get our attention. Perhaps this is because we have become casual in our relationship with him, forgetting that we are servants as well as sons, or because we allow ourselves to be distracted by the myriad things which we regard as essential. Sometimes God has to take drastic action in his great love for us, by allowing sickness or even bereavement to occur in order to get our ear. He intends us to be great, and he knows that we need to hear his directions in order to achieve that greatness, so he stops at nothing to gain our attention. What courage and persistence! What ruthless love!

My wife and I often help to teach deaf Christians. It may well be necessary to switch lights on and off or wave a hand in front of them in order to get them to stop what they're doing and fix their eyes on us so that we can speak to them. Then we, and they, have to make sure that they have heard us aright. All this necessitates earnest attention and much 'listening' on their part, but how else can they learn?

Hearing God

It is very important for us to hear God for ourselves, as well as through our leaders. Many leaders are godly people, and we should not be afraid of them, but some may be very authoritarian, expecting unquestioning obedience to what they say, whether we believe that their guidance is right or not. I suggest that we reject such counsel and find our own from our Father. I am not encouraging rebellion, but I am advising caution and sense.

We should expect God to speak to us—after all, he is our Father! If we expect him to speak to us, then he will;

but he wants us to listen carefully so that we hear correctly. By hearing, I do not mean the casual response given by the average child when told it is bedtime. Such children do not respond very quickly the first few times they are told, but when their father's voice takes on a certain tone, they suddenly seem to hear, and they arrive upstairs with remarkable rapidity.

God our Father does not care to waste words, and nor is he pleased when his children give only cursory attention to what he is saying to them. Scripture abounds with examples of those who heard him only partially, and those whose ears were so blocked by sin that they hardly heard him at all. Let us be careful that we do not commit the same sin. Proverbs 4:20–23 exhorts us: 'Give attention to my words; incline your ear to my sayings. Do not let them depart from your sight [and hearing]; keep them in the midst of your heart . . . Watch over your heart with all diligence.' Jesus reiterates this: 'If you abide in Me, and My words abide in you . . .' (Jn 15:7). We are to listen to God's word, and hear it correctly, but we must keep the channel open so that God can speak to us and we can hear.

George Mueller has some helpful comments to make. He writes:

> The prayer habit, on the knees, with the Word open before the disciple, has thus an advantage which it is difficult to put into words: it provides a sacred channel of approach to God. The inspired Scriptures form the vehicle of the Spirit in communicating to us the knowledge of the will of God. If we think of God on the one side and man on the other, the Word of God is the mode of conveyance from God to man, of His own mind and heart. It therefore becomes a channel of God's approach to us, a channel prepared by the Spirit for the purpose, and unspeakably sacred as such. When therefore the believer uses the Word of God as the guide to determine both the spirit and dialect of his prayer, he is inverting the process of divine revelation and using the

channel of God's approach to him as the channel of his approach to God. How can such use of God's Word fail to help and strengthen spiritual life? What medium or channel of approach could so ensure in the praying soul both an acceptable frame and language taught of the Holy Spirit? *If the first thing is not to pray but to hearken, this surely is hearkening for God to speak to us that we may know how to speak to Him.*[8] (my italics)

'I hear, I obey'

This should be a normal testimony from a devoted Christian. It is likely to be true if we meditate long and often in the Scriptures, and if we are constantly in touch with God through our prayer life. God asks us again and again to hear and retain his word, and of course, to obey it. James told his readers, 'Prove yourselves doers of the word, and not merely hearers who delude themselves' (Jas 1:22). To the readers of Revelation Jesus says, 'He who has an ear, let him hear what the Spirit says to the churches' (Rev 2:11; 3:6). Mary put it well when she said to the servants at Cana, 'Whatever He says to you, do it' (Jn 2:5). We would do well to follow her advice today.

Why is it so urgent that we hear God's voice?

The world needs the word

God sees lonely and desperate people in the world whom he could reach. If only we would listen to him and speak what we hear from him, then they would find life. Jesus heard from his Father 'a word for the weary', and he counted it such a privilege to serve his Father that he lost no time in speaking those words to all whom his Father lovingly pointed out to him. We are given the opportunity to do the same.

Listening is essential for guidance

We ourselves need to hear from God to prevent us from going astray. Isaiah 30:21 says, 'Your ears will hear a word behind you, "This is the way, walk in it," whenever you turn to the right or to the left.' But we could easily miss that voice if we are not listening. God does not shout, he is a King. How it must grieve him to look at those described in Psalm 106:13–15—'They did not wait for His counsel, but craved [for their own desires].' God gave them what they wanted, but 'sent a wasting disease among them.' True servants would have waited. Even worse were those who 'spurned the counsel of the Most High' (Ps 107:11). They did hear the Lord, but did not obey him. Does that strike a chord within you? If so, why not repent now, before you read on?

. How tragic it is when we go out of the will of God. Many a Christian worker has collapsed under the weight of uncommanded work, and some have died with their real work unfinished because they did not wait and listen to God. In New Testament times, too, there were those who were 'dull of hearing' (Heb 5:11). Such a condition is a recipe for disaster. It will cost us a lot to experience the answer to Paul's prayer for the Colossian church: 'That you may be filled with the knowledge of His will in all spiritual [not natural] wisdom and understanding, so that you may walk in a manner worthy of the Lord' (Col 1:9). But isn't this a destiny worth striving for?

The will of God is not a narrow path 18 inches wide with 10-feet walls either side to restrict us, neither are we robots expected only to respond to signals from a controller. I have said before that we walk in fellowship with an open-hearted God and Father; he certainly does have a plan for us, but it is something we should and can work out together with him.

Several years ago, when we were moving from

Liverpool, we sought God for guidance as to where we should go. I felt that we could go anywhere and God would bless us. Peggy, being less certain, felt the need of a scripture. In her reading she was amazed to find Jeremiah 40:4—'The whole land is before you; go wherever it seems good and right for you to go.' She then felt comforted and reassured that we could indeed go anywhere. We then prayed, 'Lord in your "anywhere" please show us your "particular".' The following day we received a letter from some old friends in York suggesting that we look at a house there; in the same post was a letter containing a cheque larger than we had ever had before. The result was that we moved there and God blessed us. Guidance requires co-operation, fellowship, obedience, and faith.

It presupposes that if we want to know God's will, then we must be willing to do it. Jesus said that 'if any man is willing to do [God's] will, he shall know of the teaching, whether it is of God' (Jn 7:17). We shall not know his will if we are set on our own. If we have preconceived ideas or if we are not surrendered to him or if we are not willing to choose a more difficult option in a situation such as a job change, then we cannot expect to receive the guidance of God. By the way, when thinking of a job change it is dangerously easy to look for the job first, then the house, then the church. I believe that this is back to front. It is more important to prosper spiritually than financially or commercially; after all, at the judgement seat of Christ, we are more likely to be asked about our spiritual career than our job success. Guidance to one point does not mean that we will stay there; we must therefore listen habitually, so that when God wants us to change course, we will be ready to hear and obey.

It is not only in our circumstances that we need to hear God and find his guidance. In our priestly ministry of prayer we need, like Job, to 'perceive what He would say to [us]' as we 'fill [our] mouth with arguments' (Job 23:4–5) while pursuing our high calling of interceding for the lost—and the saved too. In our 'warfare prayer' we must hear the word of authority from God before we bind or loose anything in his name. Jesus said, 'What-ever you shall bind on earth shall have been bound in heaven' (Mt 16:19). From this we can deduce that we must hear God confirm our guidance before we make too many decrees against our spiritual foes.

It is dangerous to be deaf

If spiritual deafness can cause us to miss the will of God and therefore miss our destiny, then it can also cause us to misguide others who may be looking to us for help and example, especially if we are in a position of leadership. God speaks out strongly against 'blind guides', particu-larly false prophets—and even good prophets who have become dull of hearing. In the light of the above, it is absolutely crucial that we hear clearly from God before we preach or prophesy, otherwise we could merely be verbalizing our Christian optimism or pessimism instead of that which God wants the people to hear. To mislead the people of God and introduce error is a real danger inherent in not listening to God. This warning should not lead us to conclude that we had better give up listening in case we make mistakes, it should simply make us far more careful in our prayer life.

Deafness is a terrible disability, as is blindness. In-ability to see is dreadful (I lost my own sight for a short while)—a world without colour and movement is awful, but a world without sound is at least as bad, perhaps even worse. Defective physical hearing can hamper life greatly because we are so dependent on aural instruction and stimulation. How much more disabling, then, is spiritual deafness.

Isaiah 50:4–5 implies that Jesus himself needed the Holy Spirit to open his ears when he was a man on the earth, not because sin ever blocked his hearing, but because he was a true man, experiencing human limitations and the temptations which assail us but without sin (Heb 4:15). At the same time, he 'learned obedience from the things which He suffered' (Heb 5:8). Surely one of these lessons was to learn to hear the voice of his Father above the noise and distractions of the earth—no wonder he spent so much time in the desert and on the hilltops where it was quiet. As God the Son in heaven, he was always in complete touch with the Father and the Spirit. But as a man, with all the limitations which that imposed on him, he was subject to physical tiredness, hunger, thirst and the need for sleep. He had sore feet and an aching back. He suffered the emotional demands and strain of seeing the everyday tragedies of sickness and death. In the midst of all this, he had to hear what God said to him lest he gave the devil an opportunity to kill him through uncommanded work. For instance, if Jesus had listened to the devil when he told him to throw himself down from the pinnacle of the Temple Jesus would have killed himself—God only promised to 'keep Him in all your ways' (Ps 91:11)—that is, the ways of God. The ears of Jesus, finely attuned through obedience, enabled him to hear by the Spirit this phrase which Satan missed out of the psalm.

Jesus made it quite plain that 'The Son can do nothing of Himself' (Jn 5:19); he needed the Spirit's help to hear the Father just as we do. The Lord's need was probably that of 'fine tuning', whereas ours is that of complete unblocking, but the Spirit is skilled in both. It is greatly comforting to me that Jesus has been through all the things we have to face: 'He Himself knows our frame; He is mindful that we are but dust' (Ps 103:14). He would say to us, 'I have been a man, I know the problems of hearing. I overcame all that hinders hearing God, and I am right here to help you to do the same.' Let him help us, then, to learn this holy art.

Pause and ponder

God is so patient with us; let's respond by learning to listen more carefully to him. After all, he is our King and we are his servants. It is only right that we should honour him with greater attention and obedience. Surely our response can, and should, be this prayer: 'Lord, I want to listen to you and I *will*.'

Part 3

Prophecy

19

How Does God Speak?

Learning more about listening to and hearing from God, and the importance of prayer and Bible meditation gives God a chance to train our inner ear. But how does he actually speak to mankind? If we can answer that, then we will be better able to distinguish his voice from our imagination. But before we try to answer that question, let me ask you this one: do you expect God to speak to you? You certainly should. He would hardly have endured Calvary, only to turn away in disinterest from those whom he had redeemed at the cost of his own dear Son's life. We are far too precious to God for him to do that. He wants to speak to us; he intends us to hear his voice; and he sent his Son to prove it.

Jesus plainly said, 'My sheep hear My voice' (Jn 10:27) and he sent his Holy Spirit to help us hear it, promising, 'Whatever He hears, he will speak' (Jn 16:13). Jesus longs to commune with us. In Revelation 3:20 he says, 'Behold, I stand at the door and knock; if any one hears My voice and opens the door, I will come in to him, and will dine with him, and he with me.' If we are meant to live 'on every word that proceeds out of the mouth of God' (Mt 4:4), then God is bound to speak those words to us, and he does. He does not bombard and overwhelm us with words, but he has much to share with us, if only he can get us to be quiet and still enough to listen and hear him, and if only he can convince us that he really does love to share his heart with us, and he really does want us to know his will and walk in it. Listening to God and hearing his voice reveals his guidance and his will for our situations, giving us the opportunity to obey what he says and walk in his will.

How does God speak?

When we talk about hearing God, we need to be clear as to what we mean. It is rare for us to hear audible words, although this does occur sometimes, just as it did in Bible times. I have personal experience of that. However, it is exceptional, and usually happens at times of extreme danger or need.

In Bible times God seems to have spoken audibly to man. He conversed with Adam, Abraham, Noah, and Moses. Perhaps this was because the Holy Spirit only came *to* them; he was not *in* them in the sense that he is in those who have been born again in Christ and thus share in his Spirit: 'He abides with you, and will be in you' (Jn 14:17). The spirit of God dwelling within us can speak to us by strong clear impressions in our spirit. As Paul says, 'The Spirit Himself bears witness with our spirit' (Rom 8:16).

In Hebrews 1:1–3 we read:

> God, after He spoke long ago to the fathers in the prophets in many portions and in many ways, in these last days has spoken to us in His Son, whom He appointed heir of all things, through whom also He made the world. And He is the radiance of His glory and the exact representation of His nature.

This passage infers that it is in Jesus that God speaks most clearly to the world. Jesus is described as 'the Word' (Jn 1:1). A word expresses what is in the heart of the one who speaks it—as Matthew 12:34 (Revised Standard Version) says, 'Out of the abundance of the heart the mouth speaks.' Taking up this truth, we can say that God, out of the abundance of his heart, spoke to us in and through his Son, Jesus. In Jesus, God summed all that he wanted to say to us, share with us, show us, and give us. Paul expresses this beautifully in Colossians 2:9 —'In him all the fulness of Deity dwells in bodily form.' Then, in John 1:16 we read that 'of His fulness we have all received.' What a word Jesus is to us! What a revelation of the glory of the Father! Jesus acknowledged this in his words: 'He who has seen Me has seen the Father' (Jn 14:9).

Pre-eminently, then, God speaks to us through his Son. The life and the words of Jesus Christ are the very sum of what God wants to say to us, therefore to contemplate the Son of God is to 'hear' God. We cannot really contemplate him apart from Scripture. Jesus himself said, 'The Scriptures . . . bear witness of me' (Jn 5:39). So, if we will not read the Bible, we will not hear from God. In the light of previous chapters, I need hardly enlarge on that.

God speaks through preachers and teachers

Thank God for those preachers and teachers who faithfully and powerfully bring the word to us. May God help us to listen more carefully to them so that we don't miss the very thing God wants to say. If we pray more thoroughly for those who bring us the word, they may have greater empowering to do so. And, being more sensitive to them as a result of praying for them, we may hear more clearly what God says through them.

God speaks through angels

The word 'angel' in the first three chapters of Revelation (Rev 1:1, 20; 2:1, 8, 12, 18; 3:1, 7, 14) may, according to some authorities, be translated 'pastor'. Your minister can be an angel! An angel spoke to Hagar (Gen 16:9–11), Lot (Gen 19:1), Balaam (Num 22:32), Zechariah (Zech 1:9), Joseph (Mt 1:20), and to the shepherds (Lk 2:10). It was an angel who spoke prophetically in God's name to Paul (Acts 27:23–24).

God speaks through creation

'The heavens are telling of the glory of God; and their expanse is declaring the work of His hands. Day to day pours forth speech, and night to night reveals knowledge . . . Their utterance [have gone out] to the end of the world' (Ps 19:1–2, 4). The sun by day and the moon and stars by night all 'say' that God is all powerful; who else could have made them, and who else could keep them where they are? Every created thing tells us something about God.

God spoke to the wise men both through a star in the East and the Scriptures which they had studied, telling them that his Son had been born (Mt 2:2–6). God speaks through the very make-up of the human being. Everyone has a deep longing for the realm beyond this finite one; no one really wants death to be the end. We were made for eternity, as the writer of Ecclesiastes observed: '[God] has also set eternity in their heart' (Eccles 3:11).

God speaks through historical events

God spoke clearly through the flood, saying that sin had gone too far. He spoke through his confusing of man's language, saying that men were becoming too wise in their own conceit. He spoke through the Red Sea saga, saying that he is the all-powerful God, greater than all in

Egypt. Amos, in the fourth chapter of his book, records what God said through events such as blighted crops, mildew, storms and plague: 'I gave you . . . lack of bread . . . yet you have not returned to Me' (Amos 4:6).

God speaks today through the AIDS epidemic, saying that a nation is only safe if it adheres to his sexual laws. He speaks through the increasing deserts in the world, saying that if men's greed causes them to rape the earth by plundering its resources, giving nothing back, then the death of their fellow men is on their heads. Romans 15:4 warns us: 'For whatever was written in earlier times was written for our instruction.' The events of history are writ large in Scripture, but few heed their message.

God speaks through our circumstances

Our lifetime is our apprenticeship for eternity; it is the training-ground for God's royalty. His eternal purposes for us cause him to allow difficult times to come, so that we are thoroughly trained for heaven. Lessons such as perseverance, grace, patience, humility and faith can only be learned down here. Therefore, when God allows trial and testing now he is saying, 'Let me use these circumstances to teach you things that will enable you to reign in glory.' He is not being cruel, but kind.

Paul heard God's voice in all his circumstances, and learned to be content whether he was abased (having a rough time and rejected) or abounding (prospering and not having to make tents). When Job found himself in extremity he spoke these noble words: 'Shall we indeed accept good from God and not accept adversity?' (Job 2:10). God was thus able to speak to angels and demons about Job's love and faith in him, even in great difficulties.

God speaks through dreams

It was through a dream that an angel from God spoke to

178

Joseph, reassuring him that Mary was not immoral and that the Holy Spirit had caused her to conceive (Mt 1:20-21). Later an angel warned him in a dream to go down to Egypt for safety (Mt 2:13). Jacob heard God through a dream (Gen 28:12-15). God spoke to a soldier about Gideon in a dream, and the latter was greatly encouraged when he overheard the interpretation (Judg 7:13–15).

At least two missionaries known to me have been warned in dreams to avoid a certain area at a certain time, and in doing so they preserved their lives. Many intercessors known to me have been awakened in the night through a vivid dream that someone was in danger or great need, and having prayed for that person, they learned afterwards that the dream was from God. Such dreams are not for an élite or another era; read Joel 2:28 again.

God speaks through small things

Barry Kissel shares the following insight about God's way of speaking to us through little things:

> I had always thought hearing God meant hearing an audible voice. Then I noticed that on Mt. Carmel God spoke to Elijah through a cloud the size of a man's hand. Whilst he watched it, it increased in size until it filled the whole sky. I discovered that in the quietness, the still small voice of God is at times like a tiny cloud. It comes as a seed thought or from a meditation on the Scriptures. As we dwell on this the Holy Spirit increases its meaning. He also puts the burden of the message upon our hearts so that at times we know no peace until we have preached it.[9]

How do we know it is God speaking

Our mind can play tricks on us, therefore it needs the reins of the true word of God to hold it in and steer its thought in a godly direction. Wishful thinking can intrude. We may persuade ourselves that Israel needs us, simply because we enjoyed a holiday there. Hearing a stirring message on Bangladesh, we conclude that we ought to go there to help. We meet a non-Christian girl, fall in love with her, and rationalize that she is bound to be saved through our witness, ignoring the plain word of God against the relationship. All these examples are based on actual instances when people thought they heard God, but wishful thinking and wrong motives caused them to be misled.

Our carnal desires can mislead us. A classic example of this is when adulterers justify their behaviour by saying that God gave them the desire for sex, and as it was not satisfied by their husband (or wife), God graciously gave them satisfaction through another, so therefore their action cannot be wrong (I am quoting an actual case).

Sincere but misguided friends—and even leaders— can bring us suspect 'revelation'. But there are criteria for evaluating what they say, in prophecy at least, as I show later. The devil can deceive us, for that is his nature. In the light of all this it is very clear that we must know how to detect what is of God from what is not.

How can we do this? First, as I have said consistently, our knowledge and understanding of the Bible is our most certain protection against error. King David said, 'Thy word I have treasured in my heart, that I may not sin against Thee' (Ps 119:11). The word in our heart keeps us sensitive to God's voice. Secondly, our communion with God will keep us sensitive to anything which is foreign to him. Thirdly, keeping our lives free from sin with the wonderful help of the Holy Spirit will keep our hearing sharp and attuned to God's wavelength. Godly friends are our guardians too, though we must be careful to evaluate what they say. But our greatest help comes from the witness of the Spirit with our spirit (Rom 8:14). If we trust him, he will help us to hear the voice of God. He may do this by giving us the peace of God to 'rule in [our] hearts' (NASB margin: 'act as arbiter') (Col 3:15).

So, when we are faced with the need to distinguish the voice of God from all else, let us look for that quiet assurance, that rest of heart, that witness of the Spirit, that recognition of our beloved Lord's voice, which is always in accord with the Scriptures, and the confirmation from our godly, trusted friends and leaders, that God has indeed spoken to us.

What do we do when God is silent?

There are times when God does not speak at all, and other times when he does not say much. It is at these times that we are put to the test, and God looks most keenly for our response.

In 1 Samuel 3:1 we read that 'the word from the Lord was rare in those days, visions were infrequent.' Compare Amos 8:11, which describes, 'not a famine for bread or a thirst for water, but rather for hearing the words of the Lord.' Surely we have known such times in our own experience, just as the saints of old did? We may well have echoed the cry of David to the Lord: 'To Thee, O Lord, I call; My rock, do not be deaf to me, lest, if Thou be silent to me, I become like those who go down to the pit' (Ps 28:1). This is echoed in Psalm 83:1— 'O God, do not remain quiet; Do not be silent, and, O God, do not be still.' We may share the frustration of Jeremiah who said, 'Even when I cry out and call for help. He shut out my prayer' (Lam 3:8). And we may identify with Habbakuk when he says, 'How long, O Lord, will I call for help, and Thou wilt not hear?' (Hab 1:2), and, 'Why art Thous silent when the wicked swallowed up those more righteous than they?' (Hab 1:13).

Why is God silent? We will not find a complete answer to this question in this life. Jesus says as much in John 13:7—'What I do you do not realize now; but you shall understand hereafter.' He may have meant shortly after, but I suspect it was a longer term than that. However, there are some possible answers to the question in hand.

God may be using us in a drama for the benefit of angelic watchers, as he did with Job. Paul reminds us of God's plan that 'the manifold wisdom of God might now be made through the church to the rulers and the authorities in the heavenly places' (Eph 3:10). If God kept whispering comfort, giving minute-by-minute instructions, and cosseting us against all danger and distress as one would a child, then that demonstration would not be very convincing to the watchers, who would be expecting a strong testimony of living faith and robust love.

Perhaps God is teaching us faith. Matthew relates the delightful story of the woman who argued with Jesus, who gently teased her while teaching her faith in the process (see Mt 15:22-28). Faith ventures where angels fear to tread. Faith walks where it cannot see. It trusts even when there is little ground, humanly speaking, for assurance. It keeps its nerve when God says nothing for a time. A Christian who has acquired such faith never goes back on guidance, nor does he flinch when hard tests come. He meditates all the more on the God who is utterly faithful, and presses on.

God is always silent when faith is absent. James 1:6–8 says we should 'ask in faith without any doubting . . . Let not that [doubting] man expect that he will receive anything from the Lord, being a double-minded man, unstable in all his ways.' If we need more faith we must spend more time looking at Jesus from whom faith comes. We must also ask for testing, for faith is only evidenced when circumstances demand it.

Asking for the wrong reason also brings no response

from God. James 4:3 says—'You ask and do not receive, because you ask with wrong motives, so that you may spend it on your pleasures.'

God is silent when sin separates us from his immediate presence. David reflected: 'If I regard [cherish] wickedness in my heart, the Lord will not hear' (Ps 66:18). But if we repent, he will hear us again.

Jesus said to his disciples that 'at all times they ought to pray and not to lose heart' (Lk 18:1). It is sometimes true that, although God is willing to speak to us, we prevent him by our failure to wait long enough at his throne until he speaks. A sovereign must not be told to hurry up because the person having an audience is in a hurry.

If God is not speaking to us, it could be that it is not his time to do so. We should not be fatalistic like the man who said, 'Oh well, I expect God will speak to me in his own good time if he wants to.' It is better to adopt the attitude of Habbakuk who, although puzzled and frustrated, said, 'I will stand on my guard post . . . I will keep watch to see what He will speak to me' (Hab 2:1). Elijah had to await God's moment for the rain to resume; he had to pray and wait till he heard from God, but he was not inactive meanwhile (1 Kings 18:42-45). We, too, must wait on and for the Lord. His timing is always right; has it ever failed?

The Enemy's obstruction sometimes prevents us from hearing the Lord. Daniel experienced this when he was praying for the nation. An angel, sent to tell him what was happening in the heavenly realms, said:

From the first day that you set your heart on understanding this and on humbling yourself before your God, your words were heard, and I have come in response to your words. But the prince of the kingdom of Persia was withstanding me for twenty-one days; then behold, Michael, one of the chief princes, came to help me (Dan 10:12–13).

God had responded to earnest prayer, as he always does, but the Enemy obstructed. However, this was only for a while.

When God speaks clearly to us we rejoice. When he does not we are faced with two possibilities: either we lose heart and faith, thus becoming of little use to God or man, or we obey the exhortation to 'consider it all a joy . . . when you encounter various trials, knowing that the testing of your faith produces endurance' (Jas 1:2). If we respond in the latter way we will press on and triumph whether or not we hear much from God at the time.

Pause and ponder

Jesus kept his ears attuned to his Father morning by morning (Is 50:4–5). We can and should do the same, with similar results.

20

Meditation and Spiritual Gifts

Prophecy is only one of the spiritual gifts, so I will briefly mention the others before writing specifically about prophecy itself. But first, to the heart of the matter.

'Man's chief end is to glorify God, and to enjoy Him forever' (Westminster Catechism). God wants us to enjoy him—this is the essence of our relationship with him. 'Our fellowship is with the Father, and with His Son Jesus Christ' (1 Jn 1:3). God loves our fellowship and wants us to love his. The creed and the epistle both emphasize God's desire and our destiny.

Fellowship with God enables us to know him better. Bible meditation is one important way of getting to know him and to enjoy him. It also greatly helps us to fulfil the desire in that great overflowing heart of our loving God, which is, to reveal himself to others. We cannot reveal a God whom we do not know. God has always wanted to show himself to men. In every age he sought for some to whom he could entrust some revelation of himself for the benefit of their fellows. Samuel, Jeremiah and John were three who were formed in the womb for that very purpose. Although these men were specially called apart, we too can be a means of revealing God. It was for this purpose that God gave us his Holy Spirit, and the working of that Spirit is meant to lead us into greater knowledge of God rather than mere excitement.

God has many ways of showing himself to man, for he is a God of infinite variety. He does not make two snowflakes alike, nor two people (how boring if he had). He is so great that no one method of revelation could do justice to him, and no one preacher could adequately convey his glory, nor one prophet, nor one miracleworker. Therefore he needs different men and women to convey the different aspects of his being. He showed his holiness to and through Isaiah; his compassion and grief to and through Hosea; his grandeur and creatorial power to and through Job; and his justice to and through Habakkuk. He showed himself to Moses through a burning bush; to Paul through a blinding light; to David through the glory of the heavens; and to John through glorious visions.

As well as revealing himself to us privately through meditation on the Bible, creation, preaching, circumstances, books and the lives of other Christians, he also shows himself to the world, through us, by manifestations of the gifts of the Spirit. These have either been hailed with great enthusiasm, or condemned on the ground that they are not necessary today, or that they lead to extremism. Surely the truth is that at least some of these manifestations are genuine. I believe that they are essential for our day. While we need to fear that which is false, we must also fear to reject that which is true.

If we live in times when the occult is so prevalent, shouldn't we covet the gift of the discerning of spirits? Are there no sick to be healed today? No need of miracles, faith, divine wisdom and knowledge? If the devil is working as an 'angel of light' (2 Cor 11:14) he could be working even within the most evangelical and charismatic of churches, as well as in the cults. Sadly, evidence affirms this. The prevalence of disunity, liberal teaching, immorality, power-seeking, tyranny, and pseudo gifts points to it. We are told to expect the false in the last days (2 Pet 2:1) but the existence of the false should surely point us to that which is genuine. No one counterfeits brown paper, but real notes. Our fear of false gifts must be balanced by a fear of grieving the Holy Spirit. We could incur the punishment mentioned in Revelation 22:18 if we reject what is plainly commanded in the Bible.

Some say that the gifts ceased when the canon of Scripture was completed, citing 1 Corinthians 13:10 as proof that 'the perfect' means the completed Bible, and therefore the gifts are no longer needed today. But this interpretation is very suspect, for the context indicates that 'the perfect' means our perfect understanding when we see God 'face to face.' Until that glorious day comes we need the gifts as much as ever.

Others have said that the church grew perfectly well for centuries without the gifts and therefore we do not need them today. First, however, there is evidence that they never died out altogether. They were evident among the early Anabaptists, the early Montanists, and the early Methodists, as well as among third-century Christians. Secondly, we must ask what church growth would be like without the manifestation of the gifts. People would be born again, go on in their spiritual life, and learn how to pray and study the Bible, but there would be a significant lack of wholeness and healing power. Such a church would not really equate with the one described in Scripture. Do you want the good or the best?

Others argue that love is what really matters, not gifts. In some sense this is true, for love is the essence of our faith and will remain when the gifts disappear. But the

Bible exhorts us to 'pursue love, yet desire earnestly spiritual gifts' (1 Cor 14:1). The Greek word translated 'earnestly' means something stretched to the limit—'with every fibre of our being' could be a modern equivalent. We could be disobeying this command unwittingly.

Jesus himself, who was pre-eminently a man of love, still needed the gifts in order to do his work. In John 5:19 he says, 'Truly, truly, I say to you, the Son can do nothing of Himself.' What is this but an admission that he needed the enabling of the Spirit. He did no miracle, neither did he preach one sermon, until the Spirit came upon him as opposed to within him, for he was always 'filled with Spirit.' He was endued (clothed with) the Spirit at his baptism (Mt 3:16). After this, it is recorded that all the gifts were seen in his life except speaking in tongues and interpretation of tongues. Although these last two gifts are not referred to in connection with Jesus, it is worth wondering whether, in his frequent times of communion in the wilderness, he may have worshipped his Father through them.

If Jesus did not despise any gift of the Spirit, how can we? If they are given to the church by her loving Head in order to strengthen and build her up, and if he has laid down conditions in the Bible for their manifestation and safeguarding, how can anyone who loves God and accepts the Scriptures either despise or reject them? Our completed canon of Scripture still commands us to 'desire earnestly spiritual gifts.' Not the least reason for coveting them is simply that it pleases God.

It will not do to say that the preaching of the word is the only thing that matters. God 'confirmed the [preaching of the] word by the signs that followed' (Mk 16:20). Those signs were the gifts. Preaching does indeed open up the heart as the general truth of Scripture is applied, but in the gift of prophecy, for example, specific truth and facts which could not be known by the preacher are revealed (1 Cor 14:24–25). God intends the gifts to be a wonderful confirmation of the preaching of the word, and we are foolish to neglect them.

Let's look at these gifts in a little more detail. I refer to those listed in 1 Corinthians 12:8–10.

The word of wisdom and the word of knowledge: I will enlarge on these below.

Faith: the accession of divine faith, given for a particular purpose.

Healings and miracles: these so obviously show the power of God. Although Satan can counterfeit them up to a point, God's power heals the whole person—body, mind and spirit. Satan's counterfeit healing leads to bondage, usually of the mind.

Prophecy: I deal more fully with this later.

Distinguishing of spirits: this is not mind-reading, but the God-given ability to see what kind of spirit is behind a prophecy, or a healing, or an apparent revelation. It could be the Holy Spirit, or an evil spirit, or the human spirit. Who can decide except one who is so gifted by the Spirit?

Tongues and interpretation: these two gifts are fiercely rejected by many Christians, but if they were given to us by the Lord Jesus himself, they must be good for the church and acceptable to him. Why, then, do we despise that which comes from the same blessed hands which saved us?

All the above gifts are *gifts*. They are given by grace, albeit to those who seek them earnestly (1 Cor 14:1). They are not earned by Bible meditation, neither does it produce them, but Bible meditation creates within us a spirit that is able to manifest them. It helps to produce in us that quietness of heart, that thorough knowledge of Scripture which comes through pondering it, that sensitivity to God in which we can more clearly tell what he is feeling, thinking, and wanting, and which helps to keep the channel of our spirit pure enough for him to pour through it these evidences of his power. It will help us to bring forth the prophetic word with clarity; it will enable the Spirit to bring about healing, for authority is given to the one in touch with God; it will cause us to discern quickly any spirit which is not of God; it will make sure that a tongue is given in a way which pleases and glorifies God and facilitates his working through us as he inspires us to manifest these gifts to others for their help and benefit.

It is a profitable exercise to meditate on the manifestation of some of these gifts in the Old Testament, for example, 1 Samuel 9:19 and 10:2 where Samuel manifests the word of knowledge, and 2 Kings 5:26 and 6:12 where Elisha has a word of knowledge.

The gifts of the Spirit seem to be manifested after an experience variously called the baptism with the Spirit, the filling of the Spirit, or the renewing in the Spirit. However, it is one thing to be filled with, or baptized in, the Holy Spirit, and as a consequence to manifest his gifts, but it is quite another matter to 'walk in the Spirit' afterwards, so that he can continue to manifest the gifts through a pure, sensitive and obedient spirit. Such a spirit depends quite largely on whether we meditate on the word. The Spirit of God will always lead us to the word of God. Jesus said, 'My sheep hear My voice' (Jn 10:27), meaning as he comforts, rebukes, warns and guides us. The important thing is to be close enough to hear him and loving enough to respond. We can seriously mislead God's people, for example, through dubious prophecy if we exercise gifts without the constant contemplation of his word. Scripture is described as 'a light to [our] path' (Ps 119:105), and our paths are the 'paths of righteousness' (Ps 23:3). The Bible is often described as a compass, or a plumb-line, so any prophecy, tongue etc. must be according to the Bible.

Woe unto those who lead God's people astray by adulterating spiritual gifts.

It is not my purpose to comment further on all of these gifts, for there are a number of excellent books which deal with them more thoroughly. But I do want to single out three which are particularly relevant to my subject, although none of them can be put into neat compartments, for they all overlap and intermingle. These are the word of wisdom, the word of knowledge, and prophecy.

The word of wisdom and the word of knowledge are not the accumulated wisdom and knowledge which any seasoned pastor acquires, but the sudden accession of divine wisdom and knowledge, the impartation of facts which could not be otherwise known, and the word of wisdom through which God tells us what to do about it. Some years ago in Canada, a man came to me asking for help. 'I beg you to help me,' he said. 'I keep doubting my salvation, and I have lost all faith and assurance.' I had no idea what to do, so I suggested that we prayed. After a while I felt God urging me to ask the question, 'Did you ever repent of that murderous quarrel you had with your brother thirteen years ago?' He fainted clean away! When he came round he spluttered and raged a bit, then he wept, repented and found peace. Thirteen years before, to the very day, he had tried to kill his brother with a bread knife. But after the Lord touched him he caught the next plane to the other side of Canada to make peace with his brother. In this situation a word of knowledge revealed a fact, and a word of wisdom showed us what to do about it. God plainly told this man to go and forgive his brother straightaway, then his peace would return and his ministry would be established again. What divine economy!

These three gifts are all distinct and yet they often flow together. Some people say that wisdom and knowledge are teaching gifts, but I do not believe this to be true. I believe that, out of all the wisdom and knowledge God has, he imparts some of it to a particular person at a particular time for a particular purpose. Words of wisdom and knowledge often occur during the utterance of a word of prophecy, and it is this particular gift that I want to examine more closely in the next chapter.

Pause and ponder

If these gifts are a way in which I can show the world that God is great and gloriously alive, then let me covet them so that I can manifest them and thus honour him. May my meditations enable me to do so in purity, as they keep the channel of my spirit clean.

21

Bible Meditation Enhances Prophecy

I want here to stress an important point which I made in the last chapter, namely that those who meditate deeply on the Bible are likely to prophesy with a much greater degree of purity than those who do not. There are different levels of prophecy. Some bring a simple word such as, 'The Lord says I am with you,' and if this comes with an anointing, it can be a blessing and a reassurance. Others give a word which has a sufficiently strong direction to make us sit up and take notice, and again, provided that we test it well, it can help us greatly. There are some who bring us such a word from God that we simply bow down, confessing, 'This is the Lord.' This latter sort of prophecy usually comes from those steeped in the word of God, and it is for such prophecy that I, for one, eagerly wait. If we all increased our meditation, the level of our prophesying would surely rise.

Is prophecy necessary?

God says that prophecy is necessary for building up the church. Paul exhorted the Christians in Corinth: 'Desire earnestly spiritual gifts, but especially that you may prophesy' (1 Cor 14:1), adding, 'One who prophesies edifies the church' (1 Cor 14:4). The church today needs this gift as much as the early church. It is necessary for unveiling the hearts of men (1 Cor 14:25). Indeed, we grieve the Holy Spirit if we reject this gift. There must be true prophecy to counter the false. The preaching of the Bible must be accompanied by signs (Mk 16:20), and prophecy is one of these.

Readers of this book must by now be convinced of my love of the word of God, and of my deep conviction that it is the main vehicle of his revelation to mankind. Therefore I am bold enough to suggest that the Bible may not be God's complete revelation. While stating again my belief that it contains all that is necessary to salvation, I cannot help noticing John's comment that 'there are also many other things which Jesus did, which if they were written in detail, I suppose that even the world itself would not contain the books which were written' (Jn 21:25). If we accept this truth concerning the works of Jesus on the earth, we can perhaps accept that sixty-six books cannot contain every single thing which God desires to show us about himself. Certainly the Bible is sufficient for everything pertaining to salvation, but it is not an absolutely detailed record of every single thing in the heart of God, and it is not a revelation of all that we need to know in our personal or church situations. The Bible is our only general guide; it gives the basic instructions for the Christian life, but not the personal or local detail needed by an individual or a local church. For instance, the Bible says that I must be like salt and light, but it does not tell me which garage or office I should be employed in so that I can function as salt and light. However, prophetic word can give this personal guidance.

The gift of prophecy, then, is necessary today, as long

as it is regarded as the divine underlining of the written word of Scripture, or the interpretation of its principles in a way which gives us clear understanding of how they are to be applied here and now to an individual situation. Those who despise or reject this gift of God should remember Paul's stern warning: 'Do not despise prophetic utterances' (1 Thess 5:20).

What is prophecy

Prophecy can be defined as 'words spoken under the sudden inspiration of the Spirit', which comfort, build up, exhort, warn and strengthen the church. They are generally unpremeditated, although not exclusively so, for sometimes they are given in advance and can be written down and read out. This gift does not seem to be a permanent endowment, but rather a momentary enabling for a specific purpose, except in the case of the prophet, who has a special ministry in the gift. At its highest, prophecy is the interpretation of the mind and heart of God as he views his beloved people, and sometimes as he views those who are not yet his people (1 Cor 14:24–25), or as he views his desecrated world.

Prophecy is sometimes accompanied by visions or pictures. These may be for sharing while uttering the prophecy, or only for our private intercession. Pictures are mental concepts which can be useful in illustrating a spiritual truth or a particular situation, but if we are not careful they can be made to mean almost anything, and we should be wary of making them into prophecies. Visions, on the other hand, are clear and unmistakable. You simply say what you see. They are often accompanied by a sense of awe and the presence of God. I believe that the dreams and visions referred to in Joel 2:28 are of this order. How exciting that they really are for today!

Prophecy had many effects in Bible times. Hezekiah prayed, and God answered him through Isaiah's prophecy (2 Kings 19:20); praise was expressed by prophecy (1 Chron 25:1–2); conviction and judgement came to David through a prophecy of Nathan (2 Sam 12:1–14); Paul was warned of danger by prophecy (Acts 21:11); Timothy was 'ordained' and gifted by prophecy. It all seems very valuable to me!

Prophecy has proved effectual today too. Many churches have been stopped in their tracks, redirected and wonderfully blessed by God through genuine prophecy. Men have had the secrets of their hearts laid bare through it and have been born again because of it. A woman in agony of soul, dying of a terrible disease, and full of doubts and fears, was delivered from all fear by a simple prophetic word. Some of its effects are salutary indeed. An elder, privately indulging in persistent sin, was called to account through a word of knowledge and a prophecy. He received a strong warning and an ultimatum from God through this prophecy, but he refused to repent, and died within days. I can vouch for the accuracy of these accounts, for I was there.

Just as there was false prophecy in Bible times (Deut 13:1–5; Jer 6:13; 2 Pet 2:1), there is also false prophecy about today. I once heard a prophecy given by a man who was acclaimed as a pastor. His words were biblical and his attitude all you would expect of such a man. He prophesied that God was with the assembly, and that he had come to settle their confusion over the leadership by giving them clear directions as to who should be their leaders. After he had prophesied for some minutes, I began to feel uncomfortable: there was no witness in my spirit that God was really speaking through him, and I suddenly felt very suspicious that he had personal motives in prophesying. Coupled with this I had a clear vision of a piece of paper with writing on it. During a break in the meeting I asked one of the leaders if this 'prophet' had shown him a list with men's names on it, and he replied that he had, and showed me the list. On it three men were designated as deacons, two as elders, and the 'prophet' as pastor. Asking God for help and grace, I publicly challenged the demonic deceiving spirit within this man, and he promptly fled. Later he was jailed for fraud. This man's human pride and desire for position opened the way for an evil spirit to get a hold on his life and thus mislead an entire church.

As well as false prophecy, we have to be aware of 'dubious' prophecy which has to be rejected as merely spectacular, soulish, or the verbalization of human optimism. Sadly, this kind of prophecy tends to dull the ears of people to the real thing. Familiarity indeed breeds contempt; may God forgive us for trivializing holy things. Several men have told me of prophecies given to them informing them that they should marry the woman prophesying. A man who came into a fortune was told in prophecy that he should share out the benefits. Some sick folk have had false hope given to them through prophecy. No wonder we are told to 'prove [test] all things' (1 Thess 5:21, Authorized Version). However, just because the gifts of the Spirit can be misused, producing unfortunate results, this should not make us turn away in fear from the gifts of God the Holy Spirit, for even in the natural realm good things can be dangerous if misused. Electricity, for example, is very dangerous, but what would we do without it? Are we to conclude that because it can be dangerous, we will have nothing to do with it?

Prophecy and teaching

Prophecy is not the same as teaching. A prophetic word may often come during preaching or teaching; it is suddenly interjected into the course of preaching, and the difference is clearly discernible to those who are listening. During a lecture which I gave at a certain theological college, the Lord, through a prophecy, addressed a number of the students one after another, giving counsel to one, a rebuke to another, comfort to several, and clear direction to several more. It was as if the Lord walked along the desks and addressed them. The students told me afterwards that they were intending to ask me for prayer and counsel after the lecture, but that God had done it all through the prophecy. They certainly detected the difference between the prophecy and the lecture. I should add that I had never been there before, and neither did I know any of the students.

Scripture itself distinguishes between preaching and prophecy. I am aware that the following references refer to those who have the ministry of teaching or prophecy, as distinct from prophecy given by those who have the occasional *gift* of prophecy, which Paul says is open to anyone. But I use these references just to show the difference between the two functions of preaching and teaching, and prophesying, so that we do not confuse them or amalgamate them. Acts 13:1 mentions 'prophets and teachers', and Ephesians 4:11 says that God 'gave some as prophets . . . and some as pastors and teachers.'

It will not do to try and merge the one into the other and say that the prophet's role has been taken over by the teacher's, for this contradicts Scripture. Jesus gave prophets to the church, and that church has endured beyond the apostolic age to this very day, therefore prophets and prophecy must be for today. A true preacher will be inspired; he will affect people by his preaching and they will be convicted; yet his ministry is largely from his study and exposition of the written word. A prophet will also revere and study the

Scriptures, but his ministry is likely to spring forth without much forethought. A vision will suddenly come to him, and he will describe it; words will flow forth (Hebrew: *nabi*) from his spirit, communicating to all the mind and heart of God. Even in the realm of the false, there is mentioned a difference between prophets and teachers. Peter warns us that just as 'false prophets . . . arose among the people . . . there will also be false teachers among you' (2 Pet 2:1).

If we believe that God has given us pastors, teachers and evangelists today, why can't we accept that he has given us apostles and prophets too? Can Ephesians 4:11 be split in half, one section referring to the early church, and the other to today? Although apostles and other prophets will not be of the same order or calibre as those in Bible times—no one writes Scripture now—they do have a similar ministry. However, since this book is primarily about Bible meditation, I will not stray too far from my brief.

'When you come together'

Whatever our churchmanship, we can make room for the manifestations of spiritual gifts if we are willing to do so. To refuse undoubtedly grieves the Holy Spirit. Most church services would be enlivened by a few healings and miracles, so why not give God a chance to do it? I believe that we have only achieved a balanced church life when we are manifesting the gifts of the Spirit when we meet together, either as a whole congregation or in smaller 'house' groups. Opportunity therefore needs to be given for the exercise of the gift of prophecy if our congregations are to benefit from it as God intended.

Prophecy should be weighed in the context of the body of believers, but if there is no opportunity for people to prophesy there, is it any wonder that some do so in corners? Leaders should help those learning to prophesy, for the flesh sometimes intrudes in anyone's prophesying, especially during early days. How will we ever learn to speak in purity and confidence unless we have leaders who will gently but firmly correct us and encourage us in this gift? Some churches stipulate that those who feel they have a word from God should first share it with the nearest elder who should then guide them as to whether it is relevant or not. Microphones are increasingly available in many churches to help the congregation to hear. This is a boon to the hard of hearing, but it is also very practical, for what is the point of bringing a word from God to his people if they cannot hear it, and how can it be evaluated by the elders or leaders if they cannot make it out? By the way, leaders should at least be visible to each other so that they can communicate their opinion of a prophecy just given. This should not be by a thumbs up or down, but something more reasoned. They also need to limit the frequency of prophesying in accordance with 1 Corinthians 14:29. Too many prophecies could confuse the people and hold up the rest of the meeting.

One question often asked is: 'How do I know when God wants me to prophesy?' My answer is that it varies. Sometimes we will become particularly conscious of God's presence with us, as though he is beside us, urging us to speak out. At other times we will find words within us which will not go away and which we must speak out. A lot of people find their heart beating much faster, and feel strongly that God is about to give them something to say. Some people have told me that they always get a strong tingling in their hands before prophesying; this may be genuine, but I tend to be wary of too many physical manifestations.

Bad habits in prophecy, as in prayer, need to be dealt with by the leaders. Prefacing prophecies with 'Thus says the Lord' is dangerous in the light of Jeremiah 23:25. Prophets such as Jeremiah could use this phrase because they were writing the Scripture, but none of us today is in such a position. In any case, if we use that kind of language, it does not leave us open to evaluation, or at least it can give that impression.

It is tempting to pad out the real word with impressive-sounding waffle. We can easily get carried away with our 'word' and speak words which God did not initiate. Another trait to be discouraged is using King James' English. There is no evidence that God prefers that language, so why use it?

The main responsibility for judging manifestations of gifts rests on the leaders or the more mature people in the fellowship (Acts 20:28–31; Heb 5:14). They should halt the proceedings after a prophecy of any weight, to give time to think about it, and even recapitulate it together to evaluate it and give an opinion about it to the people. In extreme cases it may be necessary to reject a prophecy completely and publicly, but this is exceptional and should only be done if dangerous or false prophecy is given. Nevertheless, we must be prepared to do this as deception increases in these last days. It is a serious matter to speak in the name of the Most High, therefore we should avoid sentimentality and partiality in our weighing of prophecies, whoever it is that gives them, even if he or she is a 'big name'. But because those who prophesy are usually sensitive people, we should be gracious as well as truthful, at the same time remembering that the Spirit is also sensitive, and that it may be better to grieve the one prophesying by a rejection of their word than to grieve the Holy Spirit by acknowledging as a gift that which he did not initiate.

Most leaders admit to a degree of nervousness when called on to weigh and even pronounce upon a prophetic word, but if that fear causes the leader to avoid the issue, then the people can be misled or confused, and the Lord will require an account from us on the day of judgement. Personally I prefer to risk embarrassment down here.

How do we judge prophecy?

We have seen above that Scripture tells us that we must weigh, or judge, prophecy. 1 Corinthians 2:14 points out that 'the things of the Spirit of God . . . are spiritually appraised.' In the light of this 1 Corinthians 14:29 advises: 'Let two or three prophets speak, and let the others [prophesiers?] pass judgement.' In 1 Thessalonians 5:21 we are told to 'examine everything carefully; hold fast to that which is good.' The Apostle John wrote: 'Beloved, do not believe every spirit, but test the spirits to see whether they are from God; because many false prophets have gone out into the world' (1 Jn 4:1).

What, then, can we say in conclusion to the above thoughts? If Jesus manifested these gifts of his Holy Spirit, so must we. If the word of God exhorts us to seek them, we should. If we refuse to do so, we must give an account at the judgement seat of Christ (2 Cor 5:10). Excesses by some in the 'charismatic' circles are no justification for refusing Christ's gifts. After all, there are excesses in the realm of criticism too. Many Christians, especially leaders, are afraid of things which they cannot grasp with their minds and things which they do not feel able to control or regulate because of their lack of experience. But fear is a sin according to the Bible – it says 'Fear not' 365 times.

I suggest that our attitude should be as follows.

We should regard the gifts as part of God's revelation to and through his body on earth. We should accept them as for our day in the light of the relevant scriptures quoted.

We should not allow fear or the excesses of some

Christians to make us reject them.

We should make room for them in our gatherings.

We should keep them in context: they are only part of church life.

Finally, we are to lovingly but firmly test everything, as I have said.

I repeat that we need not be afraid of the gifts of the Spirit. If a son asks his father for bread, will he give him a stone or a snake (Mt 7:9–11)? Will our heavenly Father give us that which is destructive? The gifts are dangerous in one sense—the Greek word used to describe the Spirit's power is *dunamis*, from which we get our word 'dynamite'—but they are never destructive. In any case, God has given us checks and balances to use, so let us treat everything as he says. If we feel a thing is wrong, let us refuse it; if we are not sure, let us examine it until we are; if we judge that it is right, let us accept it, enjoy it, and benefit from it.

The word of God in Scripture is the canon (straight-rod) by which we judge all these things. In Hebrews 4:12 we read that 'the word of God is living and active and sharper than any two-edged sword, and piercing as far as the division of soul and spirit . . . able to judge the thoughts and intentions of the heart.' Because man has a soul as well as a spirit, it is possible that the mind, or imagination, or feelings can intrude upon our prophecies —that is why we must be so careful in evaluating them. Our objective in judging them is the health and safety of the body as we seek to distinguish the true from the false or the fleshly. Bear in mind that a prophecy can pass some of the following tests and yet still lack inspiration.

Criteria for judging prophecy

(1) Does it agree with Scripture? We must go to the word for confirmation (Is 8:20). Prophecy must not con-

vey what a man thinks, but what God says (2 Pet 1:20). Nothing must be added that is unscriptural (Rev 22:18–19).

(2) Does it exalt Jesus? The Holy Spirit will always focus on the pre-eminence of Jesus (1 Cor 12:3; 1 Jn 4:2).

(3) Does it build up, exhort and console (1 Cor 14:3)?

(4) Is it given in love (1 Cor 13:2)? Is it given in a way which allows it to be judged?

(5) Does it witness with our spirit (Rom 8:16)? Is it Jesus' voice we hear (Jn 10:27)?

(6) Is it rightly timed, and is the person calm and controlled (1 Cor 14:32–33)? (I have known people trying to prophesy during the sermon!)

(7) Is the person speaking from prior knowledge of a situation (2 Cor 4:2)? 'Adulterating the word of God' can mean prophesying on the basis of information already gleaned by ordinary means, and using that to bring emotional pressure to bear on a person or a church. However, prophets do sometimes have to do this—for example, Jeremiah.

(8) Is the person speaking beyond his or her anointing (Rom 12:6; Eph 4:7)? People can veer away into their own imagination (Jer 23:16), and their personality can intrude. Although God does not abolish our personality —contrast Amos and Isaiah—it must not intrude.

(9) Is the word fulfilled (Deut 18:22)? Bear in mind, though, that some prophecy is long range. Some of Jeremiah's words have still not been fulfilled.

(10) Does the person's life add up (Jer 23:14; Mt 7:15–20)?

May this book encourage us to prophesy with an even greater degree of purity and a greater sense of privilege, and to judge prophecies with greater love and accuracy.

Pause and ponder

If Jesus offers me gifts, asking me to eagerly desire them, especially prophecy (1 Cor 14:1), I must not spurn them but receive them. They are meant to strengthen his church, so my rejection of them could weaken it.

22

Some Prophecies

Many prophecies have been given in recent years, some of which are particularly important for the church's health. I have included here only those which were given to me, and they are only a few of those given to me through the years. I have not chosen mine because I consider them superior to others, nor do I despise or reject those given by others; it is simply that I know exactly what I said and I am prepared to take responsibility for them. They have been carefully weighed by a large number of godly people, and their opinion is that they are still relevant, that they need repeating, and that they should be published. The following prophecies were given during or after extended times of prayer and meditation, mostly during Prayer and Bible Weeks. I offer them as an exercise in weighing prophecy, but also in the hope that they may help to mobilize the church. Further prophecies have been given to me since the date of the last one recorded here, but I do not feel it is timely to share them in this book.

From the very beginning of my experience in this gift, I have always prophesied in the first person: I knew no different because no one had prophesied in my hearing before. I hope this will not cause problems for anyone, but I do not see how I can alter what I believe God gave me. I always preface prophecies given to me by saying, 'I believe God is saying this to us; will you test it please?' So, as you read the following prophecies, I ask you to evaluate them carefully before God and accept what you can and reject what you can't.

York, 1974

I believe that God has this to say to us. There is little joy in my heart as I see your nation and the dark cloud above it; soon its underside will be tinged with red from the fire which shall fall on the land. My hand, which was once upturned as I lifted, supported and exalted it, is now downturned and I will crush and bring low because the leaders have led the people into sin. Oh that men would join their tears with mine, or do men think that I have an unfeeling heart? Once this land was great—from it I sent people to be ambassadors to give light and order to much of the world, but now, because it was great, great is its fall which I am bringing about as part of my judgement on it. See my hand in all this.

She who was mistress of much of the earth is now fallen and ravished by any foul spirit. These evil powers have raised up strongholds in the land; who will rise up and contend against them? Who will lay siege to them, watching and praying, weeping, but persevering until they fall? I look for those who will become mighty intercessors, for hollow are the foundations, and strength is diminished in the land; light will not easily be rekindled in it. Strongholds will not fall at the mere touch of a finger. Your prosperity is gone and even the people of God will suffer, being greatly hindered. They will yet need to share their bread with one another.

But, I have not left myself without worshippers. Before the holy ones in heaven I witness to the worship, faithful preaching, and joyful obedience of many in this place. There are great gaps in the Enemy's ranks because of the effective work of my people; great, therefore, is the reward laid up for them. But now, as you have known the heights, learn the depths too. My people have laughed and sung, and rightly so; learn also to weep and mourn as the priests I have made you. Put one hand in mine, and the other on the damned and the desperate. Plead their case, and share the pains of God on their behalf, and add to your reward by so doing.

I do not entreat now, I command. My hand is extended to you in love with the scars which prove it, but it holds the sceptre, for I am the King of all. I will now tear down the facades by which you deceive your fellows; none will escape my grasp, none shall hide behind another, none be anonymous, nor a sightseer. Some will withdraw from the fight because of the cost of obedience to this word, and they will know my judgement, even to the shortening of their days. Be warned; repent before the sun rises so that I do not have to carry out my judgements. Rebuild the family altars, teach the word of God, guard the homes, maintain their unity and holiness, remove all that hinders unity in this congregation that I may be able to use you to heal the land.

Let the shepherds emerge and really lead the people of the Lord. Let them speak and not be silent, quell the turbulent, and check the sightseers, so that there may be health and strength in the body. Great will be God's pruning, but it will bring the results he desires.

Worthing, 1975

It seems to me that God wants to say something to us; please listen and judge. The spirit of harlotry is deep within this nation. As I look on my own church for a bride fair and chaste, I see there harlotry, sin and every form of indiscipline. This grieves me deeply and causes the holy ones in heaven to be amazed that I do not immediately and fully judge those who perpetrate such wickedness. So I am opening the way for my judging angels to come, and I am giving liberty for powers to damage the land because it has rejected my protection. I also bring judgement to my own church because of its sin and hypocrisy.

There are those in the land who, with skilful words and with the touch of the pit, are bringing about those things which cause chaos and bloodshed. The blood of its inhabitants will stain its streets when the land is given over to the tyrants, some of whom will then come fully into view. They are not all in the one party, not on the same side; some are so skilfully covered that they are not seen at all, even in the ranks of those who are called brothers and sisters. In the ranks of those who appear to lead the people of God they will be revealed.

I tell you of things to come so that you will hear and respond. I want to make your land a demonstration again of that which is good; one that owns and honours the law of God. Alas, it has become a demonstration of that which is from the Enemy, of that which comes when every polluted thing is not only permitted but made legal by the leaders of the land. I will judge them heavily, while allowing the nation to come to the edge of destruction.

Yet my ears are wide open to any cry arising from my people. I move along the ranks, looking earnestly into the heart to see if there are those who will stand in the gap; those who will deal severely with sin, heed my word, and obey it instantly; those who will embrace the ruggedness, heat and strife of real war; those who will praise me when everything within them cries out that they should not do so. I look for rugged children who will allow my knife to go deep, who will shut themselves up and be quiet enough to sense my grief and my desires. Take out the sword and wield it, cutting to pieces the Enemy so that he is crushed and defeated, and so that I can bring you the peace and safety I desire you to have.

Do not think of years of safety, so imminent is my judgement unless I find those who qualify to be saviours of the nation.

Leaders' conference, Ashburnham, 1978

I believe God wants us to hear these words. Please evaluate them for me, brethren. Because you have drawn near to me, I will draw near to those of you who are leaders of my people, and I will lay my hands upon you with some weight. I will begin to enforce my government in every aspect of your lives. I share with you that I am so sickened by the state of my church, that I rise up in anger and say before all heaven that I will have my government within the lives of those who are called by my name. Therefore I put my hands upon your shoulders to gain your attention, to restrain a little, to make you listen carefully to what I want to say to the people. How will you speak to them if you do not hear what I say to you?

I am examining your lives with my sharp eyes which miss nothing, and I will require great cleanness in your lives from this day; I have always desired it in you, and I will now insist upon it. I will watch to see whether you devour my word, or whether you read it in a desultory fashion. I will listen closely to your conversation and your heart cries on behalf of others. I shall require you to pray concerning those who bring error into my church, and who give a wrong example, so that a way is made for me to judge them in severity. I will give them a chance to repent, but if not I will begin to remove them from the earth.

Understand, my beloved ones, and I do call you beloved, it is not beyond me to remove even you from this scene if you will not adhere to my word. I am tired of indiscipline, carelessness and messages; tired of desultory prayers, and fluctuating obedience. I require these stringent standards from you because I want to show the world a picture of my church as it should be, and not the shameful testimony it gives me now. The powers of darkness mock and accuse because of my church's failure, and I ask you to give them a clear and resounding answer through your pure lives. My dear people, my deep love is for you; my eternal purposes include you—make sure that you hear my words of love, as well as the stern things I say. Make your hearts my throne room, in which I can sit comfortably and from which I can govern your entire lives. Rise to the glory of your privileges; do so now—do not leave it all until eternity. If you love me, let it be seen through your obedience.

Ireland, 1978

I love Ireland, and have ministered here many many times, but Englishmen preaching in Ireland run the risk of seeming either to patronize or criticize. I do not want to do either of these things, I simply want to submit the following to its people.

I saw a clear vision in which the Lord came to his land of Ireland and looked at it with great yearning in his heart. There seemed to be a real weariness in his face and a look of disgust as he surveyed the events of the years here. Then he rose up and decided to do something about its situation.

I saw a broad golden band right across the whole

country. It did not divide North from South, it divided
the history of Ireland from one era to another, the past
from the present. When I asked God what it meant, he
showed me that the golden band comprised young
people in the main, though not exclusively. As I watched
them I was struck by their vigour, but then some dark
figures appeared, and I understood that they were the
parents and relatives of the young ones, and some of the
relatives claimed to be Christians. They went up to them
and began to speak strongly to them, whispering and
pointing. They became more and more insistent, shaking
the shoulders of their children and looking increasingly
vicious. I understood that they were trying to pass on all
the old rumours in order to keep them current.

The young people began to shake their heads
vigorously and to push their parents away. At that
moment some evil spirits began to attack the young ones
and some were killed, but others drew swords and waged
tremendous warfare against these demons who were by
then helped by evil princes. As the godly ones prevailed,
demons ran screaming into the darkness from where
they came. Then God said in a loud voice, 'An end to all
this viciousness carried on from generation to
generation. I will end it.' But the terrible thing to me
was that these so-called Christian parents had cursed
their children in the name of Christ. The Lord took note
of what they had done and, turning in terrible anger,
took some away by death, as if to say, 'I will not stand it
any longer.' Then I heard a great cry from the young
people saying, 'We need to know more, we must know
more, but who will teach us?' And it seemed that God
was looking around for those who would go to help. He
called some who had been well seasoned in war, those
who had been trained in the quiet places for years, and
he sent them to help.

Then the vision disappeared, and when I asked why,

God said that it had not yet been accomplished. When I asked him when it would be accomplished, he said, 'Cause my people to bring it into being by their intercessions. Lay the burden of the land upon them so that by their prayers they will prepare the way of the Lord. Then I can come and accomplish what I am determined to accomplish. Lay it upon the people of that land.'

Southend, 1980

I am saying loud and clear, pull down the strongholds of the Enemy for they are an offence to me. I want the jeers of demons to be stopped, for they are an affront to my name. Therefore my people must mobilize and be the army which I always intended them to be. Let the different companies mobilize together and learn to plead before the great God of all the earth, for no one can make a decree until he has learned to plead first. Companies are needed to bring down the great powers of darkness through decrees which God will ratify in heaven as he hears them.

If the fearful and weak will not take his hand and venture into the battle, let them stand aside and not hinder those who, knowing their inability, decide to take hold of God's ability and move against the wicked one. Let the cowardly and the apathetic ponder the judgement seat of the Lord and the account which he will require there.

Although his words are strong, God wants us to sense his love behind them. His purpose is to make us great in the great eternal kingdom. His plans transcend time: death is not the end of his dealings with us, but merely a veil through which we joyfully pass so that we can rule and reign with him for ever without limitation and in the bliss of complete satisfaction.

In the light of these things, let God's shepherds watch

with renewed vigilance over his people because of the rise of deception on a scale unknown in history, and because of the failing love of so many who name his name.

Look up into the face of God, it is shining in majesty, glowing with love, warm with desire for that love and obedience freely given by his devoted people, though tinged with anger when he sees those who only want to share his blessings but not his battles. How shall we respond to his gaze? With joy or shame?

Part 4

Final Focus

23

Jesus Our Example

As always, Jesus is our supreme example in the Christian
life. Peter said, 'For you have been called for this purpose, since Christ also suffered for you, leaving you an
example for you to follow in His steps' (1 Pet 2:21). Not
only are we to follow his example in our response to
suffering, but in everything else, including his perseverance in such disciplines as reading, studying and
meditating on the Scriptures, and hearing God through
them. Jesus quoted from twenty-two of the Old Testament books, which is not surprising considering his
devotion to them, and understanding of them, even as a
boy (Lk 2:46–47). He clearly heard from God (Jn 5:19,
30); surely this was a result of his long study and meditation on the Scriptures?

Jesus is also our example in prayer (Mt 14:23; Lk 6:12,
28). When others slept or enjoyed the comforts of home,
he would be away with God, deep in prayer, seeing
things from a heavenly perspective. His prayer and
meditation enabled him to know his Father's will in
detail, so that when he said in Gethsemane, 'Thy will
be done' (Mt 26:42), he knew exactly what he was talk-

ing about. Out of his meditations came his profound and personal understanding of such Old Testament concepts as the Messiah, the Son of man, the servant of God, and the blood of the covenant. Small wonder that this discipline of the Son of God resulted in such understanding and such powerful manifestations of the spiritual gifts in his life.

Jesus is an example of courage and determination

Isaiah said of him: 'He will not be disheartened or crushed, until He has established justice in the earth' (Is 42:4). Jesus had a definite objective and he never deviated from it, whatever the cost. Isaiah also said of him: 'I have set My face like flint' (Is 50:7). Flint is one of the most unyielding of minerals, and it well illustrates the attitude of the Son of God towards holy disciplines and against iniquity. He set his face firmly against the awful temptations from Satan in the desert, and did not yield to any of them. He set his face towards his Father's plan, so that even the terrible agonies of Calvary could not deter him from accomplishing the will and desires of his Father.

In Hebrews 12:2 we read that 'Jesus . . . for the joy set before Him endured the cross, despising the shame, and has sat down at the right hand of the throne of God.' The fact that he sat down indicates that the job was finished. John authenticates this when he records the great shout of triumph from Jesus: 'It is finished!' (Jn 19:30).

Jesus' example was an effective example

Jesus persevered in all things, and triumphed. In doing so he inspired the apostles, such as Paul who wrote in 1 Corinthians 9:24—'Run in such a way that you may win.' Many, many Christians throughout the ages have been inspired to endure imprisonment, torture, and loss of home and property because they loved and followed Jesus. Prayer and Scripture enabled them to endure, persevere and overcome. Jesus is well able to help us do the same today. Why not ask him to enable you now?

Jesus' example must not be ignored

I believe that Jesus is calling his church today to follow him and thus be a truly militant church. Nothing else but radical obedience to his example will deal with the rampant sin in the world and prepare for his coming again. For too long we have preached an easy believism and a casual commitment to Christ. Judgement and righteousness have been unpopular doctrines, played down in order to make the gospel attractive. Hell is never heard of in many churches, despite the fact that Jesus said more about it than heaven. Discipline in the church is either neglected in case it upsets the members, or it is overplayed by those power-hungry leaders who are quite willing to lord it over God's heritage. Immorality is rife among God's people, and his standards are much neglected. Some, though thankfully not all, of its leaders are like those mentioned by Hosea: 'The princes of Judah have become like those who move a boundary' (Hos 5:10), referring to those who push aside God's limits on behaviour in order to get their own way and indulge in their empire-building.

Mercifully, God is not taken by surprise in all this, and he always has some people who are obeying him. Jesus is building his church, and no one can stop him. Hundreds of new congregations are forming, and thousands of new Christians are being added to them, so there is no need for defeatism. But there is a tremendous need for realism, and it is for this that I plead.

218

Jesus, the leader of the church, is passing down our ranks today on a tour of inspection. He is insisting that we get fit and armed and active. He wants us as warlike as he is, and equally intent on his great business. But what does he see? He sees and rejoices over the strong and active congregations whose members joyfully obey him; he delights in the harvest of souls being reaped today; he enjoys the victories wrought in his name by his intercessors. But there is another side to the story. Many Christians wearing half their armour, and some with none at all, flabby followers who disgrace the name of their Lord by their unfitness for his war. He hears many of his people arguing over doctrine while many perish through ignorance of the truth. He sees leaders fighting for supremacy over each other, as though Alexander's empire is up for grabs. He sees some of these petty tyrants causing church members to be thrown out or frozen out of the congregation because they have a mind of their own and cannot be cloned. All this plays right into the hands of the devil whose motto is 'Divide and conquer'. I marvel at the patience and courage of God, who waits patiently for the church to become the strong, united, skilled fighting-force he always intended it to be, so that he can send his Son from heaven to crush the evil one for ever and lead us into the glory of everlasting day.

If we really desire to be those through whom God can work, we must set to in real earnest to become men and women of the Bible, mighty in prayer, strong in the spiritual gifts, beautiful in holiness, rugged in war, and outstanding in devotion to our beloved Lord and Master. There is no time to lose: we must start, or restart, *now*. May this book help us to know God and to serve him well.

Pause and ponder

With such a guide as Jesus Christ I need never wander.
With such a mighty champion I can overcome. With such
an example I can gladly follow. The Holy Spirit longs to
make me like Jesus, and he is able. I will never get what I
only wish for, but I can have anything that I really want.

Notes

Chapter 1

1. Tony Castle, *The Hodder Book of Christian Quotations* (Hodder and Stoughton, 1982), p. 160.
2. *Ibid.*, p. 161.
3. *Ibid.*, p. 47.

Chapter 6

4. From a short pamphlet by James McConkey.

Chapter 8

5. Roger Steer, *George Mueller's Experience of God* (Hodder and Stoughton, 1985).

Chapter 13

6. A.T. Pierson, *George Mueller of Bristol* (J. Nisbett, 1899) pp. 138-141.

Chapter 17

7. *Ibid.*, pp. 148-150.

Chapter 18

8. *Ibid.*, p. 141.

Chapter 19

9. Barry Kissel, *Walking on Water*, p. 122.

God has feelings too

by Alex Buchanan

How do you see God?

A demanding tyrant, unapproachable and aloof?

A spiritual benefactor perhaps, but one who doesn't really want to share his heart?

'I grew up watching my P's and Q's as far as God was concerned, longing to love him but too afraid to get near enough to do so... I wanted to get to heaven but rather dreaded to be for ever with One who was thrice holy and knew me through and through. I longed to know God but didn't know how.'

In this book Alex Buchanan shows how God revealed his own heart to him through Scripture and through personal experience. In his warm and natural style he shows how much richer our relationship with God can be when we understand more about God's compassion, his grief, his joy, his anger and his love.

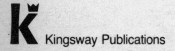

Kingsway Publications

Come into His Presence

by John Wallis

Everyone seems to agree that prayer is at the heart of the Christian life—as essential as the air we breathe—but how many Christians actually enjoy prayer?

This book has been written to remind us just how exciting prayer can be. John Wallis has seen what has happened in Korea and other parts of Asia when Christians take prayer seriously, and he longs for a similar dedication in the hearts of Christians in the West.

In a series of short chapters the author gives practical suggestions on a wide variety of issues related to both individual and corporate prayer.

John Wallis is the Director of the Overseas Missionary Fellowship in the UK.

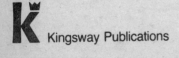
Kingsway Publications